Strengthening
Teacher Education

C. Peter Magrath
Robert L. Egbert
and Associates

Foreword by Terrel H. Bell

Strengthening Teacher Education

The Challenges to College and University Leaders

Jossey-Bass Publishers

San Francisco • London • 1987

STRENGTHENING TEACHER EDUCATION
The Challenges to College and University Leaders
by C. Peter Magrath, Robert L. Egbert, and Associates

Copyright © 1987 by: Jossey-Bass Inc., Publishers
433 California Street
San Francisco, California 94104
&
Jossey-Bass Limited
28 Banner Street
London EC1Y 8QE

Library of Congress Cataloging-in-Publication Data

Strengthening teacher education.

(The Jossey-Bass higher education series)
Bibliography: p. 167
Includes index.
1. Teachers—Training of—United States.
2. Universities and colleges—United States—
Curricula. I. Magrath, C. Peter. II. Egbert,
Robert L. III. Series.
LB2165.S66   1987   370'.7'10973   86-46336
ISBN 1-55542-037-0 (alk. paper)

Manufactured in the United States of America

The paper in this book meets the guidelines for
permanence and durability of the Committee on
Production Guidelines for Book Longevity of the
Council on Library Resources.

JACKET DESIGN BY WILLI BAUM

FIRST EDITION

Code 8713

The Jossey-Bass
Higher Education Series

Contents

Foreword   xi
    Terrel H. Bell

Preface   xv

The Authors   xxi

**Part One: Higher Education's Stake in the Preparation
of Teachers**

1. Causes for Concern About Teacher Education   1
    C. Peter Magrath

2. Reexamining the University's Role in Educating
Teachers   12
    J. Myron Atkin

3. The Importance of Higher Education to
Teacher Effectiveness   22
    Dennis O'Brien

Part Two: Strategies for Improving Teacher Education

4. Strengthening and Maintaining the Pool of
Qualified Teachers   36
    David G. Imig, Douglas R. Imig

5. Attracting Better Students to Teacher Education   55
   Henrietta S. Schwartz

6. Developing Existing Education Faculty   71
   Edward R. Ducharme

7. Redesigning the Curriculum in Teacher Education   87
   David C. Smith

8. Identifying Resources Needed to Improve
   Teacher Education   97
   Robert L. Egbert

**Part Three: Recommendations for Higher Education
Leaders**

9. What College and University Presidents Can Do
   to Strengthen Teacher Preparation   110
   W. Ann Reynolds

10. Building Campus-Wide Support for Teacher
    Education   122
    Linda Bunnell Jones

11. Enhancing the Status of the Teaching Profession   135
    John W. Porter

12. Establishing Partnerships Between Schools and
    Teacher Training Institutions   150
    Richard C. Wallace, Jr.

    Epilogue: Sharing the Responsibility for Reforming
    Teacher Education   163
    C. Peter Magrath, Robert L. Egbert

    References   167

    Index   175

Foreword

A Nation at Risk, the 1983 report of the National Commission on Excellence in Education, focused attention on the need for reform of America's schools. Among the issues highlighted in that report was the necessity for improving the manner in which teachers are prepared. Almost immediately leaders in teacher education began to formulate responses to the growing concern about the quality of programs to prepare teachers. One of the constructive steps taken was the formation of a National Commission for Excellence in Teacher Education, under the leadership of C. Peter Magrath and with Robert L. Egbert as staff director. As Secretary of Education, I was pleased to assist this commission with partial funding for its work.

In 1985 the National Commission for Excellence in Teacher Education issued its report, *A Call for Change in Teacher Education,* the first national report devoted primarily to teacher education. I agree with the recommendations of that report and with the assumptions underlying them. In particular, I believe that teachers are professionals and should be accorded the respect—and the remuneration—received by other professionals and that their education should be broad, deep, and rigorous. Such an education can best be provided by our colleges and universities—if those institutions do not relegate their teacher training programs to second-class status. To ensure that the education of teachers receives the attention it merits, the authors of this volume have addressed their chapters primarily to college and university presidents and chief academic officers and to their boards.

The authors of the individual chapters in *Strengthening Teacher Education* have equally strong identification with teacher education. Most of them were either members of the National Commission for Excellence in Teacher Education or were associated with its work in some other way.* Among the chapter authors are the chief administrators of four universities and university systems, the superintendent of a large school system, a chief academic officer of a large university system, and six teacher educators. Each of these authors brings special expertise to the topic, and each has written a chapter that will be directly useful to college and university administrators.

Campus-level administrators make a number of critical decisions about programs, including whether a particular program will be offered, what resources will be available, and who will administer the program. Some teacher education faculties will need prompting from their presidents to bring about any reforms in their programs. College and university presidents also strongly influence the value that other members of the academic and lay communities attach to teacher education and the support they give to it. Because of their important role in all major functions of their institutions, college presidents and their academic vice presidents will be central figures in any successful attempt to reform teacher education. Without their support, even the most competent and forward-reaching faculty will be limited in the improvements they can make.

Therefore, since our schools are central to our democratic ideology and are also essential if we hope to recapture an edge of intellectual vigor that many Americans believe has been eroding, I urge college and university presidents and other administrators to give serious consideration to the recommendations contained in this volume. As noted in Chapter Nine, "If presi-

---

*Members of the Commission were: C. Peter Magrath, Chair, J. Myron Atkin, Frank B. Brouillet, John Brown, Steve Cobb, Mary Futrell, Robert D. Graham, Mari-Luci Jaramillo, Jonathan Messerli, Howard C. Nielson, Joan Parent, Ann Reynolds, J. T. Sandefur, Sister Michelle Schiffgens, Albert Shanker, Mark Shibles, Richard C. Wallace.

dents, academic administrators, deans of colleges of education, and the entire university faculty . . . do not seize the initiative on our campuses at this time, the alternatives are clear. There will be increasing legislation, and increasing numbers of state agencies will regulate teacher credentialing. . . . We in higher education can do something about recruiting and developing the well-prepared teacher. The responsibility clearly rests with us."

Salt Lake City, Utah   Terrel H. Bell
March 1987   *Professor of Educational*
                                           Administration
                                           University of Utah

To Diane and Gretchen

Preface

As mentioned by Terrel H. Bell, former Secretary of Education, in his foreword to this book, *Strengthening Teacher Education* is designed to give guidance to college and university presidents and vice presidents and to their governing boards as they set priorities, assign human and material resources, and decide how they will commit their resources, including their own time as educational leaders. It is also intended to assist them in establishing priorities for their teacher education faculties. Despite the numerous studies and reports that have been written about schools, teachers, and teacher education, ours is the first volume to be directed explicitly to high-level campus administrators. We believe that it will also prove useful to teacher educators and others who are directly concerned with how our nation's teachers are prepared.

Although our book is direct—at times it is almost prescriptive—it does accommodate alternative perspectives about teacher education. For instance, although both David Smith (in Chapter Seven) and Richard Wallace (in Chapter Twelve) advocate that five years be spent in the preparation of teachers, Smith recommends a five-year, integrated program in which most of the formal course work would take place on campus. Wallace, on the other hand, believes that the student should first complete a four-year liberal arts program, containing some professional orientation experiences, before entering a fifth-year internship, which would be accompanied by academic work jointly taught by teacher educators and teachers in the schools. These differing perspectives reflect something of the turmoil that teacher education faces today.

Part One of this book describes the problems and dilemmas faced by teacher education and provides a context for understanding them. In Chapter One, C. Peter Magrath introduces the book's central issue: "The issue, stated bluntly, is the quality of the teacher in the classroom—an issue that is directly related to the quality of our programs for recruiting, educating, and sustaining our teachers." In this connection he provides specific recommendations for essential changes in the environment surrounding teachers (changes in the pay, working conditions, and status of teachers) and in teacher training programs (for example, the establishment of a five-year curriculum and a full year of internship, along with programs to attract older students and former teachers who have left the profession). He recommends, in short, not only changes in the programs themselves but also "a fundamental social and political commitment . . . to upgrading the status of our teachers."

J. Myron Atkin, in Chapter Two, begins by asking whether prospective teachers should continue to be educated in colleges and universities or whether—as is sometimes recommended —they should be trained in programs that are essentially apprenticeships. Then, through a series of rhetorical questions and reasoned responses, he concludes that education is a field of knowledge as well as practice and, as such, needs a structured setting for transmission and exploration. Moreover, he emphasizes, "a teacher, at least in the vision projected here, must be an educated person—a person aware of what a life of the mind is like."

In Chapter Three, Dennis O'Brien, borrowing an image from Plato's *Republic,* divides education into parts and stages: "primary school—aesthetic; secondary school—practical; college —theoretical." He argues that, because each stage of education should prefigure the next, a college or university president's interest in teacher education should go far beyond ensuring that the next generation of freshmen can read and figure: "The failures in crossing the segments of our divided line in education are not merely technical failures of grammar and fractions; they stem from our failure to understand the meaning of higher education as the pursuit of truth and wisdom."

Part Two deals directly with teacher education programs and faculties and the resources that they require. David G. Imig and Douglas R. Imig, the authors of Chapter Four, discuss the considerable problem of attempting to forecast the need for future teachers. Current projections, they note, "have indicated that soon there will be a shortage of qualified teachers"—a shortage amounting to a "national crisis." However, they point out, because of research problems, the validity of these projections is questionable. Nonetheless, "there is no doubt that the country is faced with a pervasive and overwhelming shortage of minority teachers," as well as "spot shortages in certain subject areas and in certain geographical regions." To remedy such shortages, they recommend that "policy makers designate teaching as a profession and give teachers both more autonomy and more responsibility."

Given the often-stated need for bringing abler people into the teaching profession, higher education must become more imaginative and aggressive in recruiting prospective teachers. In Chapter Five, Henrietta S. Schwartz recommends twelve initiatives that universities, teachers, and public agencies can pursue to attract competent students to teacher education.

Edward R. Ducharme, in Chapter Six, tells why faculty development programs are needed for teacher educators and makes nine specific recommendations for presidents, vice presidents, and other institutional leaders to consider in promoting faculty development.

Chapter Seven contains detailed descriptions of the components of a proposed curriculum designed to prepare fully qualified teachers. The program suggested by David C. Smith, the chapter's author, is sophisticated and wide ranging. He urges college and university presidents and chief academic officers to "exert leadership to help college faculty and administrators understand . . . the necessity to design new teacher preparation programs that will equip the teachers of the twenty-first century to educate youth so that they can function effectively in the Information Age."

In Chapter Eight, Robert L. Egbert emphasizes that decisions to improve teacher education, if they are to have practical consequences, require a clear institutional commitment of money and other resources, including the time and attention of the president and the academic vice president.

Part Three explores issues of particular concern to presidents and vice presidents, including the role of the president in supporting teacher education. In Chapter Nine, W. Ann Reynolds asks, "What is a weary college or university president to do" in order to recruit promising people into teaching "in a climate of intense criticism of the teaching profession and of increasing conservatism and materialism?" She believes that a great deal can be done if the president is willing to take the actions that she recommends—for instance, establishing partnerships with public schools, developing a good accreditation process, and giving more attention to the generally neglected prospective elementary school teacher.

Linda Bunnell Jones, in Chapter Ten, echoes a former president of Harvard University, James B. Conant, in calling for teacher education to become an all-university responsibility. She urges academic leaders to establish a Council for Teacher Education—composed of deans, department heads, and faculty in arts, sciences, and education—to recommend policies that will ensure "the all-university approach" to teacher education. She also recommends "a new, broader concept of the role of dean or director of the school of education."

Chapter Eleven focuses on ways of building the status of the teaching profession. The chapter's author, John W. Porter, proposes that "college and university presidents assume responsibility for helping to restore the prominence of teaching in American society." He suggests specific ways that campus leaders can enhance teacher education programs, change the public's perception of teachers, and make teaching a dynamic and rewarding profession.

Chapter Twelve, by Richard C. Wallace, Jr., presents the perspective of the superintendent of a major school system about how colleges and universities should work with schools in the initial preparation and continuing education of teachers. Wallace emphasizes that "teacher development is a continuous process, and . . . the responsibility for its progress must be shared among teacher training institutions, graduate schools of education, and local education agencies.''

In the Epilogue, we discuss our personal concerns about teacher education and the continuing flow of reports about education and teacher education. We also summarize the steps that we think are needed to improve what is being done in this area.

March 1987   C. Peter Magrath
                                                                 Columbia, Missouri

                                                                 Robert L. Egbert
                                                                 Lincoln, Nebraska

The Authors

C. Peter Magrath is president of the University of Missouri and professor of political science. He received his B.A. degree (1955) from the University of New Hampshire in political science and his Ph.D. degree (1962) from Cornell University in the same field. He holds honorary degrees from Brown University and the University of New Hampshire.

Magrath taught at Brown University and held senior executive positions at three other universities—the University of Nebraska, the State University of New York at Binghamton, and the University of Minnesota—before moving to Missouri in 1985. In addition to writings in American constitutional law and history, he has written extensively in the field of higher education, including chapters in the volumes *The Future Academic Community* (J. Caffrey, ed., 1969) and *Higher Education Surviving the 1980s* (G. H. Budig, ed., 1981).

He has served as a director of the federal Board for International Food and Agricultural Development, as chairman of the National Association of State Universities and Land-Grant Colleges, and as chairman of the Association of American Universities. Between 1984 and 1985, Magrath chaired the National Commission for Excellence in Teacher Education.

Robert L. Egbert is George W. Holmes Professor of Education at the University of Nebraska-Lincoln. He received his B.S. degree (1947) from Utah State University in psychology and his

Ph.D. degree (1949) from Cornell University in educational psychology.

Egbert has taught at Utah State University and Brigham Young University and has worked in educational and psychological research for the New York State Education Department, the Human Resources Research Office, and System Development Corporation. He also directed the Follow Through Program for the United States Office of Education. Prior to his current assignment, Egbert was dean of Teachers College of the University of Nebraska-Lincoln for eleven years. He has written on subjects in the fields of education and psychology, recently focusing on teacher education. His publications include *Using Research to Improve Teacher Education* (with M. M. Kluender, 1984) and "The Practice of Preservice Teacher Education" (*Journal of Teacher Education,* 1985). He has been involved in teacher education for more than twenty-five years.

Egbert has been president of the American Association of Colleges for Teacher Education and has served on its board of directors. He also chaired the external review panel in the 1985 recompetition of the United States Department of Education-funded Regional Education Laboratories. In 1984-85 he was staff director for the National Commission for Excellence in Teacher Education.

J. Myron Atkin is professor of education at Stanford University; from 1979 to 1986, he was the dean of education there. From 1970 to 1979, he served as dean of the College of Education at the University of Illinois at Urbana-Champaign. He received his B.S. degree (1947) from the City College of New York in chemistry and his Ph.D. degree (1956) from New York University in science education. He currently serves as senior adviser to the National Science Foundation for programs in science and engineering education.

Edward R. Ducharme is professor of education at the University of Vermont, where he chairs the Department of Organizational, Counseling, and Foundational Studies. He received his B.A. degree (1955) from Colby College in English, his M.A.T. degree

(1956) from Harvard University, and his Ed.D. degree (1968) from Teachers College, Columbia University. He has written widely on secondary schooling, staff development, teacher education, and preparation of higher education faculty.

David G. Imig is executive director of the American Association of Colleges for Teacher Education in Washington, D.C. He received his B.A. degree (1961) in social sciences, his M.A. degree (1964) in history and political science, and his Ph.D. degree (1969) in foundations of education from the University of Illinois at Urbana-Champaign.

Douglas R. Imig is a doctoral candidate and teaching assistant in the political science department at Duke University. He received his B.A. degree (1984) from St. Mary's College of Maryland in political science and his M.A. degree (1986) from Duke University in the same field.

Linda Bunnell Jones is dean of academic programs and policy studies for the California State University. During the past three years, she has been responsible for a variety of initiatives to improve teacher education programs on the nineteen campuses of the California State University. She received her B.A. degree (1964) from Baylor University in English and her M.A. (1967) and Ph.D. (1970) degrees from the University of Colorado in the same field.

Dennis O'Brien is president of the University of Rochester and is also a professor of philosophy there. Before moving to Rochester, he was president of Bucknell University (1976-1984). He received his A.B. degree (1952) from Yale University in English and his Ph.D. degree (1961) from the University of Chicago in philosophy. He holds honorary degrees from Wilkes College and Middlebury College. O'Brien's books include *Hegel on Reason in History* (1975) and *God and the New Haven Railway* (1986); he has also conducted research on the history of higher education. He is a member of the boards of LaSalle College, Union Theological Seminary, and the Commission on Independent

Colleges and Universities (New York). He also serves on the Presidents' Commission of the National Collegiate Athletic Association and on several corporate boards in Rochester.

John W. Porter is president of Eastern Michigan University, Ypsilanti. He received his B.A. degree (1953) from Albion College in political science, his M.A. degree (1957) from Michigan State University in counseling and guidance, and his Ph.D. degree (1962) from Michigan State University in higher education administration. Porter taught in the Albion and Lansing school systems for five years and has served as associate superintendent of the Bureau of Higher Education of the Michigan Department of Education (1966-1969). In 1969 he was elected state superintendent of public instruction by the Michigan State Board of Education—the first black state school superintendent in the United States. He has published many books and articles relating to education and has served on several state and national commissions and advisory boards.

W. Ann Reynolds is chief executive officer of the California State University, the nation's largest system of four-year and graduate-level higher education institutions, with nineteen campuses, 325,000 students, and 36,700 faculty and staff. She received her B.S. degree (1958) from Kansas State Teachers College in biology and chemistry and her M.S. (1960) and Ph.D. (1962) degrees from the University of Iowa in zoology. Formerly provost of Ohio State University, and associate vice chancellor for research and dean of the graduate college at the University of Illinois Medical Center, Reynolds is an award-winning scholar in developmental biology, specializing in studies of fetal development, placental transfer, and nutrition. She is the author or coauthor of more than one hundred scholarly works.

Henrietta S. Schwartz is dean of the School of Education and professor of administration and education at San Francisco State University. She received her B.A. degree (1950) from Northern Illinois University in English, her M.Ed. degree (1966) from Loyola University (Chicago) in educational administration, and her Ph.D. degree (1972) from the University of Chicago in anthropology and educational administration. She has written extensively on a variety of subjects, including multicultural education and equity, ethnography and cultural pluralism, and teacher and administrator stress. A member of several professional organizations, Schwartz has had a broad range of administrative experiences at the secondary level; has taught courses in anthropology and education, curriculum development, and principles and practice of administration; and has administered a variety of research, evaluation, and applied programs.

David C. Smith is professor of education in the Department of Educational Leadership and dean of the College of Education at the University of Florida. He received his B.A. (1954) and M.Ed. (1958) degrees from Northern Iowa University and his Ph.D. degree (1966) from Northwestern University in educational administration. Before assuming his present position, he was a high school teacher and principal and the dean of education at the University of Montana. He has also served as volume editor of *Essential Knowledge for Beginning Educators* (1983).

Richard C. Wallace, Jr., is superintendent of the Pittsburgh Public Schools. He is also an adjunct professor in educational administration at the University of Pittsburgh and a research associate at the university's Learning Research and Development Center. Pittsburgh is widely recognized for its vigorous achievement-monitoring and staff development programs. The Schenley High School and Brookline Elementary School Teacher Centers reflect the district's intense commitment to revitalizing its teaching force. Wallace received his B.S. degree (1953) from Gorham (Maine) State College in sociology, his M.Ed. degree (1960) from Boston College in administration, and his Ed.D. degree (1966) from Boston College in curriculum and instruction.

Strengthening
Teacher Education

1   C. Peter Magrath

Causes for Concern
About Teacher Education

One central issue needs to be addressed by all those committed to improvement in American education at all levels. The issue, stated bluntly, is the quality of the teacher in the classroom—an issue that is directly related to the quality of our programs for recruiting, educating, and sustaining our teachers. Education in the nation's schools, in short, can be no better than our teachers. Put another way, the quality of teachers, the quality of education in the schools, and the quality of teacher education are inseparable.

      Our nation's schools are not, of course, a disaster area. We are blessed with many excellent teachers in our elementary and secondary schools. Nevertheless, these schools are poorer than our country deserves and needs for the intensely competitive period that is already upon us and that will persist as we move into the twenty-first century. Similarly, our teachers, often underpaid and undervalued, need and merit commendation, not condemnation, from those of us who profess concern about the quality of the American educational enterprise. An especially compelling matter that must be addressed turns on the question of access and opportunity for all students and, most particularly and explicitly, the diverse ethnic and minority groups that enrich our population.

Because the questions involving our teachers and teacher education programs affect virtually all Americans and legitimately lend themselves to public debate and involvement by our politicians, there are dangers involved. The dangers arise because there is no single, simple problem involving our schools, teachers, and teacher education programs—and therefore no single, simple solution to this critical and complex challenge. Here surely is an arena of public discussion where the old principle *caveat emptor* should prevail: the buyer, ultimately the American citizen, ought to be very careful indeed about buying simple solutions, quick fixes, and dramatic overnight cures. Simple and easily packaged, ready-to-implement solutions promise something that they cannot deliver and therefore lead to frustration when the promised changes do not materialize rapidly, causing at worst a total withdrawal from engagement with the social problem and, at the very least, temporarily diverting attention from the real task.

Our real task is to work, in careful but determined ways, to improve the teaching of teachers and therefore the quality of education in our nation's schools by public discussion, evaluation of new programs, and a willingness to experiment in our various states, school districts, and colleges and universities. There is a need for response and follow-through to the slate of serious and thoughtful proposals offered by Boyer (1983) on behalf of the Carnegie Commission on Higher Education; the proposals of the Holmes Group (Lanier and others, 1986), representing a number of education college deans; such other books as *A Place Called School* (Goodlad, 1984); and the findings and recommendations of the National Commission for Excellence in Teacher Education (1985).

The significant and deep-seated change that is essential if our schools and their teachers and teacher education programs are to be truly upgraded will not, however, come about if the resources necessary for quality teacher education do not materialize. The proposals in recent reports—and indeed in this book itself—will prove to be meaningless rhetoric if significant investments are not made in both our teacher education programs and the teaching profession. This issue, of course, is both subtle and simple. It is simple in that fiscal resources must be invested in teachers and teacher education programs; but it is subtle in that such investments will not occur if we do not match our words with deeds and give high status to our nation's teachers and the critical work that they do. On a national average, the investment made by educational institutions in the graduation of a professional teacher must be comparable to the investment made in the graduation of a professional engineer. At present the average cost of educating an engineer is approximately 50 percent higher than the cost of educating a teacher. All citizens, and most particularly our leading politicians and public officials, must accept responsibility for improved funding for teacher education if the objective is to improve the quality of education in schools at large.

Changes Needed in External Environment

To be sure, good programs and imaginative curricula and innovative ideas are essential; but that is insufficient unless adequate resources are assigned to teacher education, so that the very best teacher trainers can work with the very best teacher candidates in thorough and rigorous programs. If it is a correct assumption that teacher education programs are directly linked to the quality of our nation's schools and the teachers within them, then the public and its leaders must firmly insist that fundamental changes be made in the pay, working conditions, and status of teachers; otherwise, the essential foundation for improvement of our teacher recruitment and teacher education programs will not be created. The external environment in our schools must be significantly improved in at least four ways:

1. Teachers' responsibilities and working conditions should be commensurate with the requirements of the job.
2. Administrative leadership within the schools should be much more emphasized and enhanced, so that school principals and superintendents—who play key practical and symbolic roles—can provide instructional leadership and

create the conditions that will nurture the profession of teaching.

3. Teachers should be given professional development opportunities and incentives, so that they can consistently improve their teaching.
4. Teachers' salaries should be increased to levels commensurate with salaries in other professions that require comparable training and experience.

These changes reflect a national dilemma: teaching in our nation's schools is a profession, but it is an undervalued and underpaid profession. Although many states and localities are attempting to upgrade the shameful—and costly—low status of teachers as measured by the profession's poor salaries, the need goes far beyond establishing better salaries for truly good teachers. Equally critical is the establishment of programs and procedures through which teachers can improve their status and rewards as their experience and contributions grow over the years. True, teachers can improve their salary by an almost mechanical acquisition of college credits and advanced degrees, but that is hardly the same as the development of a reward system based on actual, demonstrated experience and performance in a classroom. In turn, far too many teachers lack professional autonomy in decision making, thereby being discouraged from exercising creativity in the teaching process. There is also an insidious fallout from the low professional status of most teachers; for *their* pupils in our elementary and secondary schools surely learn a subtle lesson about the true status of the teaching profession, so that many of the best and brightest of these students are unlikely to consider teaching as a profession to aspire to— unlike medicine, law, or engineering, to name but a few high-status professions.

A particularly distressing symptom of the profession's low status and the frustration level of our teachers emerges in this startling fact: approximately half of all new teachers leave teaching within five to seven years. In North Carolina, for example, a study (cited by A. K. Campbell in the *New York Times*, Aug. 28, 1985) revealed that two-thirds of those who had scored in the top 10 percent of the National Teacher Examination had left teaching within seven years. Does this happen with doctors, or lawyers, or even college professors, who reportedly are currently somewhat demoralized?

Changes Needed in Teacher Education Programs

These, then, are some of the external or environmental conditions that affect teachers and teacher education programs in our nation's schools. But certain direct challenges also must be faced by colleges and universities with teacher education programs—challenges that cannot be postponed until some magical transformation takes place in the external environment. Colleges and universities that choose to operate teacher education programs must consider and confront changes in those programs. Underlying such changes is the need for an institutional commitment to teacher education as a critical mission of the college or university—as critical as graduating liberal arts students, top-ranked graduate students with prestigious doctoral degrees, doctors, dentists, and lawyers, or, for research universities, producing research and obtaining research grants that bring public prestige and recognition. Part of this institutional commitment requires an integration of effort between colleges of education and colleges of arts and sciences, an integration premised on the assumption that teacher education is a responsibility of the total college or university. One of the tragedies of American teacher education, which is perhaps now on the way to being corrected, has been the separation and division of effort between the faculty in colleges of education and the professors in arts and science departments. This separation, in fact, virtually mirrors the relatively low prestige attached to teacher education programs and, ultimately, the teachers in our nation's schools—environmental and external conditions that have already been noted. Unless our best and most dedicated teacher education faculties join with their colleagues in the arts and sciences, the prospect for sustained curricular improvement in teacher education programs, and for the attraction of the highest-quality students into these programs, will not come to fruition.

Those who propose changes in teacher education can easily produce their own list of what needs to be done in effecting curricular and programmatic changes. My list of critical changes includes at least four components:

1. A much stronger liberal arts component in teacher education programs and the establishment of a five-year curriculum.
2. The establishment of a full internship year for prospective new teachers following the completion of their academic studies.
3. The development of new relationships between teacher education programs and the elementary and secondary schools, in which teaching exchange programs between teacher educators and teachers in the field become an operative day-to-day reality.
4. The development and intensification of programs to provide new stimulation and upgrading for teachers in the field and to provide entry into the profession for prospective older teachers or for former teachers who have left the profession (usually because of frustration and dissatisfaction with working conditions).

Strengthened Liberal Arts Component and Five-Year Curriculum. Although many critics wrongly assert that the nation's teacher education programs are foolishly focused on teaching methodology at the expense of academic content, there is significant room for strengthening the liberal arts or subject-matter component of teacher education programs. All those who enter the teaching profession ought to have an academic concentration in a genuine liberal arts curriculum, receiving an education in which the requirements in the arts and science subject matter are clearly equivalent to a bachelor's degree. All teacher education programs, even the very best, need to be improved. Students majoring in education "need at least as much knowledge of the subject to be taught as an undergraduate liberal arts major possesses. They need special knowledge in understanding how students learn concepts in a subject and what to do if students have problems learning the material. Further, teachers need considerable practice in real situations where their work is constructively criticized" (National Commission for Excellence in Teacher Education, 1985, p. 11).

If this high standard is to be met, and if our prospective teachers are to learn how to be effective teachers, a five-year curriculum leading to a master's degree is imperative. This was the view of a majority of the members of the National Commission for Excellence in Teacher Education (1985, p. 15): "First, we contend that one cannot be liberally educated without in-depth study in at least one academic subject. All prospective teachers, as part of their liberal education, should be educated in at least one academic major. This is as true for the person who will teach first grade as it is for the person who will teach high school physics. Second, we believe that the kind of teacher education program proposed by the commission cannot take place within the usual four-year baccalaureate. A minimum of four years should be devoted to the liberal arts component of the teacher education program; a minimum of five years to the total program."

Obviously, this reform has costs attached to it. Lengthening teacher education programs to five years keeps the prospective teacher from the employment market for approximately one year longer. It also involves institutional costs, and it implies that the new teacher, once fully certified and in the field, will be remunerated in proportion to the additional effort he or she has made—a remuneration, of course, that ought to be consistent with the push to improve the professional status of teachers, the quality of our nation's schools, and the environment in which teachers work.

A Year of Internship. The second change that ought to be made, and it follows logically and naturally from the strengthened liberal arts requirement and the five-year teacher education program, is that all prospective teachers should have a full year as a teacher intern after completing their teacher education program. Under this change prospective teachers would receive a provisional teaching certificate upon completing their teacher education program, and they would then work as teachers at full starting pay—but clearly as interns still under probation.

This period of internship would be in addition to the field experience that prospective teachers currently receive under "practice teaching" programs and would be equivalent to a full-scale professional apprenticeship analogous, say, to that experienced by medical doctors. Such an internship period symbolizes the seriousness of entry into the teaching profession as a prized achievement; it gives interns an opportunity to determine whether they really want a career in teaching, recognizing that, as beneficiaries of a strong liberal arts education program, they have other options available to them; and it allows school districts to assess the new teacher as a prospective permanent employee. Relatedly, and of course under the assumption that teaching is indeed a significant *and* demanding profession, the internship period provides a further opportunity for the teacher education programs, in collaboration with the school district, to monitor and assist the new teachers.

New Relationships Between Teacher Education Programs and the Schools. The third programmatic change that should be pursued by colleges and universities devoted to significant change in teacher education is the exploration of new and imaginative relationships with the elementary and secondary schools. To be sure, teacher education faculty already work with practice teachers in the elementary and secondary schools, supervising their performance and helping them with curricular matters. But many of these efforts are routine and, although important in and of themselves, do not accomplish what could be accomplished if new ties were forged between teacher education programs and the nation's schools. Faculty in our teacher education programs should not only teach undergraduate students at the college; they should also (at least some of them) serve as teachers in the elementary and secondary schools. Similarly, the best teachers in the elementary and secondary schools could serve as teachers of undergraduates majoring in education. Such arrangements, indeed, could be structured as a sabbatical reward system for outstanding elementary and secondary school teachers, who would in turn profit from the stimulation involved in a return to a lively college or university atmosphere. Yet another idea that could be explored would be the use of teaching teams made up of college and elementary and secondary teachers to further a shared approach to teacher education involving the actual field laboratories—the nation's elementary and secondary schools—and the colleges of education. Both in practice and symbolically, such linkages would make the point that there is an indispensable relationship among all levels of education.

Programs to Attract Older Students and Former Teachers. Finally, our teacher education programs must make direct provision, as some are already doing, to develop paths by which older students can be encouraged to acquire the skills necessary to become teachers. Not everyone who has had interesting experiences in life, even those with sound academic credentials, can or should be a teacher. However, much more can be done to attract promising students who are older than the traditional college-age student into the teaching profession. Programs for such students—which would not, of course, need to be the traditional four- or even five-year degree programs—could add numerous excellent teachers to the profession, thereby helping to meet the nation's teaching shortage. An upgraded teaching profession and a heightened attention to teacher education programs in colleges and universities also could attract the many excellent teachers who left teaching after only a few years. Such college programs—aimed at providing both methodology and strong liberal arts content to prospective teachers who are not traditional college-age students, as well as to potential reentering teachers—might be regarded as alternative teacher education programs, but their quality could and should be as high as that of the more sequential teacher education programs. As the members of the National Commission for Excellence in Teacher Education (1985, p. 20) commented, "The fundamental differences between the alternative and the traditional program is the audience and the training design, not the content, the rigor, or the expected outcomes."

Methodology Versus Content in Teacher Education

As changes are contemplated and made in teacher education programs, it is important to keep in mind that teaching is a complex science—and an art. Those who suggest that courses on "how to teach" and methodology are meaningless and should be eliminated from teacher education curricula are wrong; teaching combines both art and science, and while it must first and foremost proceed from a strong and rigorous base of academic content, a teacher must know how to communicate that content. Moreover, our nation's new generation of teachers must have knowledge of how one teaches students of different ages and backgrounds and how one helps students overcome difficulties and errors. If teacher education courses in methodology are poor and weak, they should be eliminated, just as any academic course that is weak and shoddy deserves elimination. But to throw out the good teaching techniques with the bathwater of poor methodology programs would be the ultimate disservice to the pupils in our elementary and secondary schools.

Moreover, just as our teachers must be well grounded in teaching methodology and in the knowledge of diverse student audiences, so too must they benefit from a solid base in organized educational research, research that contains vital information about teaching and that can be documented on the basis of practical experiences. Moreover, if it is foolish to assume that all the problems of our nation's elementary and secondary schools can be "solved" through the application of technology, it is equally foolish to discount the importance of technology and the use of computers and other educational technologies in the schools. Whether one likes it or not, contemporary society is profoundly influenced by technology, and the imaginative integration of technology into teaching ought to be a prime component of teacher education programs—yet another reason, incidentally, why a five-year curriculum for teacher education is imperative.

Conclusion

If the recommended changes are made in our teacher education programs, and if a fundamental social and political commitment is made to upgrading the status of our teachers, then surely our nation's schools will be substantially improved. The appropriate watchword is quality in standards, but it must be quality in standards consistent with the American ideal of openness and equal access for all students, including our rich and diverse minorities. Teaching is a profession, but the unhappy truth is that the teacher is not yet a fully vested professional in our society; the derivative truth is that the teacher education programs in our colleges and universities reflect this underserved and ultimately costly second-class status ascribed to teaching, teacher education, and our nation's schools.

Perhaps the low status of teachers, teacher education, and ultimately our schools reflects a paradox. We do place a high value on education; for we argue about it, have political fights over it, and give it great media attention. Why, then, on the average, do we fund it so poorly? Is it because, as a people, we are still consciously governed by that old and vicious prejudice "Those who can, do; those who can't, teach"? Yet is not the contrary the truth: that those who *can* teach effectively are among the nation's most important doers? We must act soon on this fact and reassess the value we place on our schools, our teacher education programs, and our teachers, both in word and in deed.

2   *J. Myron Atkin*

Reexamining the University's Role in Educating Teachers

What kind of an occupation must teaching be to warrant university-level preparation? Is it an occupation that requires intelligent application of well-understood and more or less standard practices to specific situations but does *not* require a wide range of choices, informed judgment, the display of taste and values, adaptation to particular circumstances, the practice of intellectual inquiry, the assignment of priorities to competing goals, or knowledge acquired through reflective study? Is little more than supervised experience needed to enter the field? In short, if teaching is something like plumbing, or TV repair, or flying an airplane, with a clearly demarked and singular way of reaching an unambiguous goal, then we may do well to relinquish the role of the university, any university, in teacher preparation.

Note: This chapter is adapted from remarks first prepared for the National Commission for Excellence in Teacher Education and subsequently delivered to the Holmes Group of Deans of Education at Wingspread, Racine, Wisconsin, in June 1985. The Wingspread statement appeared in the *Wingspread Journal,* Summer 1985, and in *Basic Education: Issues, Answers, and Facts,* Vol. 1, no. 3, 1985, published by the Council for Basic Education.

In comparing teaching to a demonstrably skilled craft (and plumbing, flying, and TV repair are all unquestionably sophisticated skills) that does not require a college degree, one need not be accused of creating a straw man. There are clear indications that the occupation of teaching is moving in such a direction. Teaching is increasingly rule directed: by legislators, by state education agencies, and by the producers of instructional material. Look at "Individualized Education Plans" demanded by congressional legislation, or the increasing use of externally imposed examinations required by the state, or the growing popularity of highly prescriptive textbooks. To the extent that those who set policy for educational practice continue to move in such a direction, it becomes continually more questionable whether the university should play a major role. To learn the rules and the prescribed practices, teachers could be prepared as other skilled craftsmen are: in a program lasting a few years beyond high school. Whether or not such preparation should be associated with a degree—as contrasted with a certificate attesting to the completion of the program and demonstration of the ability to function in a classroom—is another matter. This point is not probed in depth here, but the possibility at least should be contemplated, if only to sharpen thinking about teacher education and what a university is all about.

There is no logical reason for associating state licensing requirements with academic credit. Universities often have been too casual in awarding credit for work that may be perfectly reasonable as prerequisite to a teaching credential but is inappropriate for university-level study: observing in schools (without being required to analyze what one has observed), for example, or learning how to run a movie projector or to program a microcomputer. If teaching is a highly regulated activity, with goals delineated unambiguously and narrowly, learned largely through experience or tightly prescribed techniques that can be acquired relatively easily by a quarter of the nation's adult population, then why should a degree be necessary?

Right now, this trend toward viewing teaching as a skilled craft seems to be seen by the public as desirable, judging from the increase in state-mandated requirements. Furthermore, it

seems to be welcomed by many teachers, by some school administrators, and even by those who prepare teachers at universities. The security of certainty about instructional objectives
and the clarity of assessing program quality when goals are specific and easily operationalized offer tremendous appeal to
many people. In fact, it seems reasonable to assume that the
occupation of teaching will continue to move along such a path
for the remainder of the decade, at least in public schools; that
is, in schools that are most directly accountable to the public
and susceptible to oversight by legislative and state education
agencies. The alternative simply may be too difficult, and not
only politically.

However, if there is to be a different model of teaching,
and if it is unlikely to be articulated by those responsible for developing laws and regulations about teacher certification or by
those employed in the occupation itself, then perhaps it falls to
faculty in schools of education to present the alternative.

Need for Teachers to Be Considered Well Educated

A vision of teaching is outlined in this chapter that is
quite different from the image conjured up by viewing the occupation as analogous to TV repair, or flying an airplane, or programming a microcomputer. I start with the conviction that
teachers, to achieve the autonomy that is necessary in the picture portrayed here, must be at least as well educated as those
whom the general public considers well educated. In view of
college-going rates in the American population these days, with
more than 50 percent of the people in many states moving on
to some form of postsecondary education, and with a higher
percentage than ever of the population earning a bachelor's degree, the operational consequence of this conviction is that
teachers should have a bachelor's degree that is considered as
rigorous as anyone else's. That is, their general education, including the academic major, should be just as strong as that required of other college graduates. In the current system of academic accounting, it takes four years to acquire a suitably broad
general education and the academic major. There is room for

other course work, sometimes a minor, usually general electives; but the bulk of the work is in the major and in meeting the general education requirement.

No defense is implied here of what passes for general education at most universities; nor, for that matter, is it assumed that the content of the academic major is justifiable. Both, in the opinion of many careful and insightful observers, need considerable revision. The public has begun to hear a great deal lately about the questionable quality of liberal education at America's colleges. Furthermore, the academic major in many fields has been unexamined for decades; it represents a virtual rite of passage toward graduate-level study in the particular discipline, often serving primarily to weed out all but the most persistent. The rite-of-passage analogy is used advisedly. Education for the teacher must be good, if possible; just as important for the point made here, it must be seen to be rigorous, difficult, and worthy (although the distinction between "worthy" and "difficult" may not be all that clear in the public mind).

One can offer an additional argument for a strong general education and an academic major. That is, in order to exercise significant judgment, a teacher, at least in the vision projected here, must be an educated person—a person aware of what a life of the mind is like. A science teacher, for example, should not be ignorant of Shakespeare; or, more pointedly, of how the political process works with respect to issues such as the teaching of evolution and environmental protection; or of the rudiments of quantitative thinking. An English teacher should be well read but also should be aware of developments in technology that affect our modes of thought; of the history of artistic expression in other than literary forms; and of the relationship between political developments and literary expression.

Some would say, some *do* say, that a bachelor's degree is all that is required for teaching. Beyond such attainment, certification by a practicing teacher or school administrator that the candidate can survive in a classroom is all that is necessary. Maybe so, but let us ask whether some additional attributes might also be attractive, even necessary. First, with respect to subject matter alone, is the undergraduate major sufficient?

I was an undergraduate chemistry major in college, taking the required sequence of courses: general chemistry, qualitative analysis, quantitative analysis, organic chemistry, organic analysis, and more. Because I wanted to be a chemist, and that seemed to me worthwhile, I proceeded through this sequence of courses on faith, without feeling particularly knowledgeable about the subject as it was conceived by those who knew it best. That is, I had no clear idea of which concepts were most fundamental, which had the most explanatory power, which were relatively transient, which were most likely to offer a foundation for future developments. I did not even think much about such questions. Like many other undergraduate majors, I did not see the conceptual forest for the trees. It was not until my twenty-fourth semester hour of chemistry, in the physical chemistry class, that the field began to reveal some coherence for me, and I began to understand which knowledge within chemistry was of most worth. I do not mean to suggest that I felt I had mastered the subject, but at least I felt I knew where to find the road map.

Maybe I was a particularly slow learner, or maybe my instruction was uninspired; but it is my impression that many undergraduate majors, in any field, do not even reach that point. It is self-evident that teachers need the kind of road map I am suggesting here. If it is not acquired during the normal course of completing the academic major—and usually it is not—then it must be acquired somewhere else, during postbaccalaureate study if necessary.

In my view, however, even that knowledge does not constitute sufficient subject-matter preparation for the teacher. There should be something else—namely, an understanding of the subject field that is aligned to issues associated with teaching the subject to youngsters. Should a teacher of physics know the most common types of difficulties that youngsters face in trying to understand the concept of inertia, or randomness, or acceleration? Should the teacher of mathematics know the three most common errors that youngsters make in learning the binomial theorem and the conceptual basis for those errors? Teachers, I believe, should have this kind of knowledge about learning a subject field if they are to teach it well in a class-room. And they cannot acquire such knowledge solely by majoring in the subject as an undergraduate or even by taking a Ph.D. in the field. If teacher educators believe that a teacher should have such knowledge, then they must contemplate a level of preparation that extends beyond a broad general education, the undergraduate academic major, and even the "capstone" courses in a field.

So far, this argument has focused on general education and subject-matter preparation only, and a program has been suggested that extends well beyond the bachelor's degree. What about work in the field of education? We can best address this question by asking about the kind of person whom teacher educators, and perhaps the public, want in the classroom.

Need for Understanding of Philosophical
and Political Issues

A teacher spends most of his or her time working with youngsters, of course. Do those interested in educational policy care how he or she views children? Should the public hope for the best, undefined and unexamined? Or should a teacher know that there have been different conceptions of the child over the centuries, from Locke to Spock, and that one's view of children has a fundamental effect on apparently so mundane an issue as the tone of a simple conversation between an adult and a child? Some key educational debates today—and undoubtedly in the future—turn on issues as basic as the contrasting educational philosophies of John Calvin and Jean-Jacques Rousseau. Should a teacher have an opportunity to probe these philosophical issues in some depth during the course of a preparation program?

Education is a field buffeted increasingly by conflicting political priorities. During the height of the civil rights movement, the schools became a major vehicle for reaching goals associated with equity. In fact, the primary institutional initiative to address what is probably America's most deep-seated social problem, race relations, was focused on the schools. The consequences for classroom life were enormous, sometimes

overwhelming. Should a teacher, during the course of a preparation program, be given an opportunity to understand the extent
to which the schools serve political and other social purposes—
what the public expects of them, reasonably or unreasonably,
beyond the transmission of factual knowledge and intellectual
skills?

The United States seems to be destined in the coming
years to hear even more about tuition tax credits and voucher
plans. Should teachers have some background that helps them
understand how schools are funded and governed, and what
initiatives such as California's Proposition 13 do to traditional
concepts of local versus state control of education? More fun-
damentally, should classroom teachers understand how the
common-school movement developed during the nineteenth
century, and what it accompanied and accomplished? Or about
the history of educational reform during the twentieth century? Formal educational institutions were not created yester-
day. Americans and others have shaped them for decades. Do
certain issues seem to arise periodically in debates about education? If so, should teachers know about these issues and learn
what has been done about them in the past? For example,
should a teacher be able to talk cogently with a local newspaper reporter about issues in bilingual education, or minimum
competency testing, or the desirability of instituting a statewide
examination that is a requirement for high school graduation?
Each of these questions has deep historic roots and profound
consequences. Should teachers know something about them beyond this morning's headlines?

Need for Understanding of Educational Techniques

What kind of knowledge must a teacher have to perform
the day-to-day tasks associated with working with youngsters in
a classroom? If the general concept of a well-educated teacher
seems desirable, then the implications for concerted study within the field of education in subjects such as educational history,
educational philosophy, political science of education, and economics of education are clear. Maybe the American public does

not care whether teachers have this kind of knowledge. But do teacher educators and educational policy makers care? If so, should the point be stressed in an attempt to influence the rapid changes taking place today in reformulating requirements for teacher preparation all over the country?

To round out this picture of the teacher, it is necessary to turn to some characteristics associated directly with the day-to-day responsibilities in an ordinary classroom. Teachers give tests, sometimes designed by the teacher, sometimes by someone else. Should we expect teachers to know something about constructing test items—specifically, that some questions elicit simple recall and that others assess more intricate mental processes and that both are important? Should teachers know whether some forms of evaluation are useful for diagnosis of an individual student's progress, others for making judgments about programs, and still others for assessment of mastery? And what about the use of test scores that result from externally imposed examinations? Should teachers be expected to know how to compare their students with others or how to make judgments about a student's progress over time?

What about instructional materials? Should teachers know about the purpose of different types of instructional materials, the effectiveness of different kinds of textbooks, the potential and limitations of devices such as worksheets and take-home examinations, the use of newer technologies, or the range of effective out-of-school learning?

What about grouping children? Are some kinds of learning best achieved by means of a lecture and recitation approach, others by the use of small groups, still others by independent research on the part of the student?

One could, and should, go on; but let us move to a different set of issues by asking whether those who educate teachers want also to develop in teachers the rudimentary ability to conduct inquiry into classroom-based problems. If a chemistry teacher has persistent difficulty in teaching the periodic table, for example, should she or he not only be aware of research conducted on the subject but also know how to initiate an inquiry about the problem? Should teachers, in short, be expected to know how to find answers to questions that arise in the course of ordinary practice and that are difficult to anticipate in a formal program of teacher preparation? In other words, is teaching an occupation in which one is expected to continue to learn? If it is, what elements should be built into a program of preparation to enhance the chances that such learning will take place throughout a career?

No one has any difficulty in adding to the list of attributes and knowledge desirable in a teacher. Do we want teachers to know about the development of unions, for example? Or about how educational systems are organized in other countries, the problems that are faced in these nations, and how they are approached? How much should teachers know about the development of children's thought, or how youngsters are socialized in school, or what role the family plays in intellectual development? Such a list is not short.

Finally, should teachers be familiar with the rich literature of research on teaching styles? Such studies compare one teaching style with another and assess the effects on what children learn. Researchers have found, for example, that teachers who manifest a certain flexibility in a classroom, instead of adhering strictly to detailed lesson plans, seem to promote independence on the part of children and favorable attitudes toward school and themselves; however, more focused teaching, pursuing fewer lines of thought than seem appealing at the moment, results in higher achievement scores on conventional tests. Another example: Considerable research evidence indicates that teachers who demand a great deal from youngsters and are somewhat critical when student performance fails to meet expectations foster higher achievement levels in their classrooms than those who do not make such demands. Stating objectives for a lesson at the beginning often enhances certain types of educational achievement but not others. One could go on; the research literature is extensive and often significant. The question: To what extent should prospective teachers study not only the outcomes of such research but the way it is conducted and the implications it might have for their own behavior once they start to teach?

Problems of Implementation

There are abundant difficulties with the vision projected in this chapter for a model teacher for the nation's classrooms. Even if we ignore challenges to the soundness of the views advanced, and undoubtedly there are more than one or two, the practical problems are far from insignificant. For example, such a program probably would take a minimum of six years to complete, at least with the present system of academic accounting, especially if one includes a desirable amount of student teaching and internship experience. If the nation were contemplating a grand total of 300,000 teachers in this image, over a decade or two, the task might not be insurmountable. But 2.5 or 3 million? How would the additional education be funded? If six years of preparation is necessary, what steps must be taken to assure that undesirable financial barriers are not erected for those who would like to teach?

There are answers to this question, at least tentative ones. But no one can be confident that the public much cares about staffing the nation's schools with people like those suggested here. A prior question, though, is whether those who educate teachers care. Maybe they do, but the local realities seem too overwhelming even to contemplate moving in the kind of direction outlined here; perhaps, for understandable reasons teacher educators will continue to accommodate to an occupation that requires just four years of preparation. If so, then I wonder whether universities, in view of the values they hold and the capabilities they work hard to acquire, should be in the business of teacher preparation at all. And if teacher education is not a central concern of the schools of education at the nation's universities, what other forms of professional preparation take its place? And if nothing does, then it is legitimate to ask, as others have, why schools of education should be funded at the university level. If schools of education are good only for studying educational phenomena—even if they are superb at it—why not make them departments in liberal arts schools, where relevant standards of scholarship are probably better applied, and there is no false expectation of relevance to a field of practice?

Dennis O'Brien

The Importance
of Higher Education
to Teacher Effectiveness

When I was asked to write a chapter on why college and university presidents should be concerned that teachers be well prepared, the first image that came to mind was the opening scene of that most famous of modern collegiate epic films, *Animal House*. As the camera pans across a bucolic campus, we see the statue of the founding president. Underneath this imposing effigy is the college motto: Knowledge is Good. Faced with the task of commending teacher preparation, one could easily imagine being cast in eternal bronze cliché. Surely, the interest of higher education in teacher preparation for intellectual and practical reasons must be so obvious that one can scarcely imagine filling a decent-sized chapter with worthy thoughts. Bad teachers mean weak students unable and unwilling to proceed beyond secondary school. Sheer self-preservation dictates an interest in preparing those who prepare our future undergraduates. However one decorates self-interest with the larger social interests in producing an intelligent citizenry or tasteful consumers, the essential connection of the levels of education suggests the most immediate interest in teacher preparation.

But if the subject is obvious and fraught with self-serving

pieties, why is the question raised at all? Do the compilers of this volume believe that university presidents and their institutions have been less than solicitous to the preparation of teachers? I expect that they do, and I expect that they are correct. To be sure, many institutions regard the training of teachers as at least part of their historic institutional mission. They and their chief executives cannot be accused of disinterest. I suspect that the problem lies elsewhere: in the leading research universities and the strongest of the liberal arts colleges. Many of our leading universities do, of course, have schools of education, which specialize in the preparation of teachers. My own university has an excellent school engaged in that task. A few of the leading four-year institutions have departments of education, and most have some rudimentary programs in education for the occasional student who abandons upward economic mobility for the calling of primary or secondary school teacher. If the truth be told, however, most institutions with aspiration (or mere pretension) are uneasy about their teacher preparation areas—whether they be schools, departments, or programs. Teacher education is not the road to academic preferment. This fact is paradoxical, not only because of the already stated self-interest that should motivate higher education but also because these institutions do not seem to lack respect for teachers at the lower levels. On the contrary, many of our most prestigious institutions go out of their way to honor great primary or secondary teachers with special medals, ceremonies, and even an occasional honorary degree. Higher education honors the teachers but not the formal pedagogies of teaching. That is the issue I wish to address.

The Divided Line: A Philosophical Perspective

I want to examine this university suspicion about teacher preparation in order to understand its philosophical base and to determine what, if anything, needs to be done to correct attitudes, practices, and institutions. In order to accomplish this purpose, I will resort to myth. The study of education is clogged with facts and data from innumerable earnest surveys and studies.

I am not a surveyor or even a historian of education, so I choose
the philosopher's ruse of telling a "likely story." My myth shad-
ows at a respectful distance Plato's famous description of the
line and the cave in Books VI and VII of the *Republic*. In that
passage Socrates begins by constructing a figure based on a ver-
tical line, which is divided in a curious fashion into four segments. The line represents the "ascent of knowledge" from
awareness of mere images to knowledge of "the forms." Socrates
then goes on to explicate the "divided line" by the famous
myth of the cave, in which a prisoner who has been chained in
darkness is released from his chains and gradually exposed to
the reality revealed by daylight.

My "divided line" also has four segments, representing in
a very rough fashion the four basic levels of educational structure in America: grammar school, secondary school, undergraduate college, and graduate and professional training. This sequence is understood, even by the general public, to be a ladder
of ascent toward greater and greater "knowledge," more perfect
skill, or some gradual accretion of the "good." Otherwise, why
would anyone continue on up the costly steps of education?
But how (if at all) are the later stages on the divided line of
American educational institutions related to the earlier? As people advance "up" the ladder of education, do they acquire some
knack or knowledge that allows them to function better when
they go on to teach in "lower" schools? (One might well recall
here that, as Plato expands his cave story, the philosopher who
returns to the cave of darkness with knowledge of reality is regarded as a blunderer by the denizens of the dark, who, of
course, know (gropingly) how to get around while the philosopher is functionally blind in that environment. One may have
to *prove* that "higher-level" knowledge really is useful in a
"lower" setting.)

Now that I have laid out my divided line and named the
parts, let me label the nature of the segments. My "stages" are
aesthetic, practical, and theoretical, and I will equate these
stages with three stages of education: primary school—aesthetic;
secondary school—practical; college—theoretical. (What is left
out is the graduate school level. It is at this level that one looks

back and makes the distinctions just suggested. It is the "meta" level of discussion, the level of professional self-reflection on teaching.)

I have chosen this particular segmentation not only for general philosophical reasons but also because of the current discussions about teaching in the lower schools. In March of 1985, the American Educational Research Association and the Johnson Foundation sponsored a Wingspread Conference entitled "Multidisciplinary International Research Symposium on Classroom Discussion as a Means of Teaching and Learning." As a university president, I found it a rare opportunity to spend several days in extended discussion with researchers and practitioners who are deeply involved with primary and secondary education. My suggested typology of the divided line of educational levels results from my attempts to understand the conflicts and arguments of that conference. I hope, therefore, that my remarks here are not merely metacomments over nonexistent issues. They are, in fact, related to some powerful guiding concepts that exist within the primary and secondary school community.

Problems with "Discussion" Theories of Education

Of the various studies presented at the conference, I was particularly grateful for the work presented by Eileen Francis from the Moray House College of Education in Edinburgh, Scotland. Many of the conference papers were careful empirical investigations of various outcomes brought about by certain techniques of classroom instruction. Professor Francis's paper, on the other hand, offered a broad prospectus on the basic aims of and appropriate methods for secondary education. The basic philosophy was *discussion,* and it was around that central concept that she and her colleagues had established a Discussion Development Group (DDG), which was intended to "transform the future education" of fourteen- to sixteen-year-old students. By expanding "discussion" to a complete educational ideology (even a complete life philosophy), Professor Francis gave depth to the empirical results. She also provided me with a philosophy of education that I could deeply disagree with; and by coming to understand the nature of that disagreement with her, I was able to construct the typology described in this chapter.

The problem I had with Professor Francis's views on the education of fourteen- to sixteen-year-olds may well be at the root of the problem that institutions of higher education (and university presidents) have with supporting teacher preparation programs. One can so construct the ideology of lower-school teaching that it seems radically discontinuous with work at the higher levels. The line is truly *divided.* One will then have great difficulty in finding the *intellectual* foundation for higher-level study of education. Lower-school teaching will be viewed, as I believe it is by many "elite" educational institutions and their leaders, as a knack of personality, not a "science" to be pursued.

The DDG model of education can be simply described, though I will not give it the careful nuance that Professor Francis would prefer. The basic thrust of this "discussion theory" of education is that it should be nonauthoritarian. The role of the teacher as primary information giver and initiator of classroom events is to evolve into the role of the teacher as resource person and enabler (Francis, 1985). The insistent nonauthoritarian mode of teaching and participatory discussion advocated by DDG rests, in my judgment, on a barely disguised psychological and political viewpoint. Avoidance of authority is beneficial for psychological self-development and political democracy. (DDG was so firmly committed to nonauthoritarian modes that its members were hesitant to participate in the Wingspread Conference because it supposedly gathered "authorities" on discussion to discuss discussion.)

Since I have already alluded to Platonic philosophy, it will come as no great surprise that I am suspicious of the DDG views—at least as a preferred or synoptic theory of education—even at the lower-school level. Plato placed the democratic state well down on his list of preferred regimes and, though Socrates is a supposed model of discussion, the *Republic* (to take a notable example) largely leaves Socrates' interlocutors saying "Agreed" or "I understand"—even when one suspects they do not.

At face value the program of DDG is very attractive and

conforms to the kind of open, democratic rhetoric favored in descriptions of "best teaching techniques" in American education. The problem lies in the unspecified outcome of the discussion. In certain constructions it appeared to me that the aim of discussion was to be a good (self-confident, democratic) discussant. Discussion is its own reward. This is not a silly option, but I believe it is highly restrictive.

If education is a divided line, it is first of all a *line*; and what makes it a line (a continuity) is that at all levels some sort of "teaching transaction" occurs. As long as we are talking about education, we should be talking about teaching, since it is teaching that distinguishes even the most advanced graduate education from a research laboratory or solitary scholarship. Let us assume that the single line of education from kindergarten to Ph.D. is some form of teaching transaction, and we can call that for short-hand purposes "discussion." Could the DDG program as quoted be a synoptic view of education applicable at all stages on the ladder of schools and colleges?

If education throughout is teaching transaction/discussion, then I would want to make a distinction between the aims of discussion by level of education. My sequence is aesthetic/ practical/theoretical for primary/secondary/collegiate. Each of these levels of education may emphasize distinctly different outcomes. The application of "discussion" philosophies proper at one level may wholly subvert the aim of another. The DDG mode of discussion is what I call "aesthetic." In this model one wishes to understand one's own opinions (and self) as well as *appreciate* the opinions and values of the other. Teachers are facilitators in a process of mutual self-understanding. Self-enhancement is encouraged as dominating authority is removed. The outcome of such discussion is values appreciation or values orientation.

The virtue of such appreciative dialogue is obvious on its face, but its limitations are severe. In itself, aesthetic education fails both practical and scientific aims, which are equally important in any general view of education. A deep structure of science that particularly clashes with an aesthetic view of education is the "suppression" of self, which is meant to be revealed in the aesthetic mode. Aesthetic education helps us to know our (inner) selves; scientific education tells us about (external) reality: the "truth." Too much talk about "the truth" may seem presumptuous to those who see extensive fallibility in even our best science. But even if it were true—which I am sure it is not—that science has no absolute certainties, the discussion of science would be a distinctively different enterprise from the values orientation of the DDG. Admiral Byrd's expeditions to Antarctica and the North Pole were distinctively different from a stroll on the polar ice cap. Similarly, an aesthetic education and a scientific (theoretical) education are both decidedly different from a practical education. Just as there is a world of difference between a scientific symposium looking for a cure for cancer and a values orientation session for varying ethnic populations, so there is a distinct difference between either and the practical *negotiation* that leads to a *decision*. I may negotiate peace and never understand your values or even care to.

A plausible argument can be made that the youngest students benefit from aesthetic discussion, whereby their sense of self is enhanced and they learn to appreciate the values of others. As one advances to the "school-leaving age," practical skills should be developed. From a community point of view, mere values appreciation will not suffice, since at some point citizens have to resolve value differences. Negotiation and decision skills are central to practical discussion. Finally, of course, one may need to know not what the other person values and how to negotiate a settlement but what is the *right* course of action, not just the negotiable one. (One imagines a variety of negotiable positions on the national debt or acid rain. But which one is the "true" solution?) To the extent that higher education is in some special manner the realm of the theoretical, one may begin to understand the uneasiness that higher education seems to display toward teacher preparation. If what the lower-school teacher "knows" is the art of enabling discussion or teaching how to negotiate decisions, is that a skill based on theory or subject to improvement by theoretical investigation and analysis? If not, then higher education will find a hard time locating the place of teacher preparation in its mansions of theory and truth.

One can construct, then, an intellectual framework to explain the curious paradox of higher education's needing teachers, applauding their performance, and yet saying, in effect, "There is really nothing we can do for you as prospective teacher. We give you subject-matter knowledge (science), but there is no science-for-teaching." There is as distinct a dividing line between lower-school education and higher education as there is in Plato's distinction between images and experience (the lower portion of the line) and true science (the upper portion). Yet it is interesting that, in Plato, the divided line is not laid out as four segments of differing length; it is constructed according to a proportion. The rationale for proportionality in the line is Plato's view that the *Republic* is describing a process of *education*: certain citizens may be moved up the line toward philosophical wisdom by proper teaching and training. The philosopher-king is not a happy accident of nature or a grace from heaven; he is a potential end product of education. Thus, in discussing the stages of knowledge, Plato must construct his diagram of advance in a manner that indicates some ratio between lower and higher; or else the movement up the line could not be the product of *ratio* (Latin for "reason"). There must be some sense of "science" even in the realm of images; and, despite initial blundering in the dark, the philosopher who descends from the light and the top of the line must be able to understand better and control the world of sensibility (the aesthetic) and the practical affairs of state.

What are the conditions that permit higher education to help lower-school education? In the first place, there has to be a sense of higher and lower. That may seem to go without saying, and yet it is inappropriate language if either the aesthetic or the practical model of discussion is the synoptic model. The aim of the DDG aesthetic model is value orientation, not practical decision or scientific demonstration. All men and women and their views are of similar value. Similarly, the practical model—although it does move beyond merely appreciating to negotiating a settlement—makes no real distinction between higher and lower. Even if one were to make "peace" the ultimate good to flow from negotiations, it is not clear that every negotiated peace is acceptable. The American Declaration of Independence (and de facto declaration of war) says "We hold these *truths* to be self-evident," and it is on the basis of such truths that a state of war is preferable to a state of peace. If higher and lower exist in education, it is because there is an assumption that sequencing exists and that it rests on theory ("truth" broadly construed) as the determiner of high/low.

If there is a sequencing of stages in education from "lower" to "higher," then the later stages must be prefigured in the earlier stages, so that the student who progresses "up" the line has a sense that the later state was something promised at the earlier. For this reason alone, some qualification on the pure DDG model of education seems appropriate. Although aesthetic education may be a predominant mode at an early stage in personal and educational development, it cannot become the sole mode if the student is to "appreciate" the practical and scientific modes yet to come. The converse of early foreshadowing should be the value of later "science" for guiding the earlier stages of education. Parity of reason suggests that higher education should have something valuable to teach us about the aesthetic and the practical modes of discussion/teaching transaction.

One obvious and immediate interest of higher education in teacher preparation, therefore, should be to imbue teachers with a sense of sequence in the *un*divided line of education from early to late. Teachers at the most elementary levels must have a sense that an educational North Pole exists and that kindergarten is an early expedition, not a ramble. Advanced training in disciplines is an obvious means of getting lower-school teachers to sense the discipline of research and evaluation, which constitutes the "scientific" mode of higher education. If colleges and their schools of education preach an aesthetic philosophy of education, then lower-school students probably will fail to understand the power of knowledge and will seek the power of material things instead. The decline in graduate pursuit of academic subject matters is not only a product of poor economic conditions in the profession; it may also result from a loss of belief in real intellectual discovery. Once the quest for our educational North Pole is lost, students may decide to abandon the rigorous climate of research and hard thought for more immediate pleasures.

In my view, then, teacher preparation should emphasize the claims for truth at the end of the road and the progressivity of the sequence of schoolings. Can it also help teachers acquire the skills appropriate to the "prescientific" aspects of education? Since I am trailing Plato in this analysis, it is fair to point out that the great master was puzzled about the question "Can moral virtue be taught?" If one assumes, as I do, that there is great positive value in the DDG model of education for the lower schools—with the qualification that science must be foreshadowed—then one must recognize that the skills of the teacher-enabler are more like moral virtues than intellectual ones. The classical Greek "four square" virtues were courage, temperance, justice, and wisdom. Certainly, it takes something like these habits of action to manage an open classroom. Fairness to all opinions, the self-confidence (courage) to be self-effacing (rather than the cowardice of dominating with obviously superior knowledge), even temper in the squabbles and "ego trips" of others—all these qualities appear to be moral traits that most university and college presidents praise in commencement addresses but do not know how to include in teacher preparation programs.

There is a powerful assumption that the moral virtues—even those of the teacher-enabler—are products not of a learning but of a training. Plato recognizes that one acquires courage not by reading essays on heroism but by placing oneself in risky situations, experiencing fear, and learning the habit of control. Practice teaching in programs of teacher preparation are, one supposes, the logical equivalent of Socrates' suggestion that the young be led to the edge of the battlefield. To the extent that good teaching comprises a set of moral habits—and I very much suspect that it does—then I doubt that higher education can contribute directly to the acquisition of the habits. Higher education is theoretical, not practical; it is learning, not training. The proper perception of the importance of *practical* virtues in teaching has contributed to the uneasiness with which university leaders view programs of teacher education.

Practical Wisdom: Higher Education's Task
in Teacher Preparation

Although I noted modern classroom analogies to the classical moral virtues of courage, temperance, and justice, I deliberately omitted wisdom. It is the science and wisdom of teacher preparation (if any) that must be higher education's task. Is there a science for education? Surely all the schools of education about the country purport to give scientific clues to sound educational practice. Sociology and psychology of learning are well-developed fields, and they purport to assist the teacher in carrying forward a successful practice. There should be no quarrel over the fact that the various social sciences have contributed materially to the improvement of various aspects of teaching practice. Yet there remains some deep insecurity about how far education can be understood as "a practical science." If one compares education science and its practice with medical science and its therapies, one must wonder whether education is a practical science at all analogous to the healing arts. If one seeks a medical similarity, education seems more like psychotherapy, a practical art that offers striking insights and suggestions about human behavior but continues to have considerable difficulty in establishing a clear-cut effective practice. Freud himself resisted the link between medical education and his efforts. A plausible case can be made that Freud was more a "moralist" than a medical man.

The "social sciences" are unlikely ever to achieve the status of physical science and practical art, and for this reason there will continue to be some dissatisfaction with education. The same problem troubles psychotherapy as a practical application of psychology. Ricouer (1980), in his study of Freud, suggests that Freud lacked the theory for his therapy or, conversely, that the therapy is better than the theory. The problem can be simply stated, though the implications are profound and extensive. Sciences—even social sciences, in which I include psychoanalysis—deal with examples; therapy deals with cases. In true science any instance must be taken as equivalent to the universal type. This frog is *the* frog. Individual history is discarded so that the individual can serve as a *specimen*. When we turn to therapy, however, we cure the individual patient. Physicians begin by taking a patient's "history." But in medical practice the history is generalized. It reveals symptoms of a common ailment: ulcers or arthritis. In psychotherapy, however, history cannot be transcended. The psychotherapist does not take the history in order to transcend it toward a general disease and its effective cure. The therapist may diagnose a case of hysterical paralysis, but the *illness is in the history*. The story that the patient tells is a history of symptoms, but it is also the disease itself (and its possible cure). As Freud said, his patients "suffered from reminiscence." The ulcer patient recounting his "history" does not suffer in and from the history. Ulcers are relatively discrete items to treat; psychotherapy treats the entire fabric of a human life.

Psychotherapy is more a practical wisdom than it is a scientific technique, and this model may be the proper one for education as well. Teacher preparation may receive support from the social sciences, but it is finally faced with a practical task analogous to that of the psychotherapist. It must act upon the student in his or her historical density. (Clifford Geertz (1973) has admonished sociologists to reconstruct the field not around universal models but on what he calls "thick descriptions." The issue of understanding an individual society is identical to the problem of treating the individual psychological case.)

If the study of education is finally a teaching in practical wisdom, can this virtue be taught any better than courage or patience can? As a philosopher by trade, I believe it can. (Not that all philosophers would agree; but then they never do.) If teaching is a combination of scientific knowledge *and* moral habits, then there is a special moment in the moral life that is subject to the ministrations of higher education. Colleges and universities are poor at training the necessary conditions for the active parts of the moral life, but one aspect of the moral life involves thinking and planning. In this sense, there may indeed be a pedagogy of practical wisdom.

The twentieth century has witnessed a curious truncation

of the moral life to the most forthright of the classical virtues: courage. The apotheosis of courage to the whole of virtue may lead us to admire the sheer guts of gangsters and goons. Morality has its "intellectual" moment when the moral person must assess the proper course of action—not just the one where he or she can be brave, but the proper course of action. In its classical mode, this part of moral life is "practical wisdom," and I believe that there is a species of instruction for it. Failure on the part of university and college leaders to believe in education in moral wisdom may well be the root failure in the disdain of teacher preparation.

Practical wisdom is not a science applying universal concepts to specimen instances. It is also not a habit of action, as courage or temperance is. It is a mode of "thoughtfulness"—surely a mode of behavior scarcely honored in the age of the thirty-second commercial. If the model for teacher preparation in higher education is confined to applied science (sociology and psychology) and moral action, then universities and their leaders may continue to regard education studies as unsatisfactory. The science does not seem to apply with great surety; moral training went out with *in loco parentis*. My own suggestion is that the model for education studies should be education in practical wisdom. Nor do I think that this is a utopian goal, such as education in sainthood.

Most of us recognize those who possess the virtue of practical wisdom. University presidents may be particularly harassed by those who lack that virtue: idealistic zealots, sarcastic depressives, and a host of types who inhabit the comic pages of academic novels. What characterizes a man or woman of practical wisdom? We have various descriptions: experience; a sense of history; a largeness of vision, seeing both before and after. Can these characteristics of practical wisdom be developed as a result of our teaching in higher education? I believe so, though there is some "leap" of mind and heart that finally congeals into practical wisdom. (Otherwise every historian would be wise —which is not really the case.) The pedagogy for practical wisdom begins in the clues from psychotherapy and Geertz's notion of thick descriptions. One must embed social science insights on education in the dense actuality of individual, national, regional, and school cultures. Education studies as thick descriptions supply the materials of practical wisdom. It is for this reason that the education school at the University of Rochester is attempting to focus its program on "the Study of Educational Institutions." Actual institutions are "everywhere dense"; they are not abstractions but named entities with specific histories and cultures.

Should college and university presidents take an interest in teacher preparation? Of course. But this interest should extend well beyond assuring ourselves that the next generation of freshmen can read and figure. The failures in crossing the segments of our divided line of education are not merely technical failures of grammar and fractions; they stem from our failure to understand the meaning of higher education as the pursuit of truth and wisdom. If neither of those ancient values can be asserted, then higher education will only be advanced skills training—vocational education with panache.

David G. Imig

4   Douglas R. Imig

Strengthening and Maintaining the Pool of Qualified Teachers

Since 1983, when the National Commission on Excellence in Education published its report, *A Nation at Risk,* we have been virtually bombarded by reports, commission studies, round tables, and hearings on the status of American education. During the years, attention has shifted from the schools and the curriculum to the quantity and quality of the teacher work force. Compensation, credentialing, and the conditions of work are now the focus of attention. Policy and decision makers have become convinced that there is a need for more and better teachers and thus have been considering incentives to attract good teachers, alternative programs to prepare them, and different staffing patterns to retain and promote them.

Like all occupations, teaching is subject to imbalances in the supply of and demand for its workers. And current projections have indicated that soon there will be a shortage of qualified teachers. In his column in *AACTE Briefs,* Imig (1986) notes that early in 1985 Dennis Doyle, then of the conservative American Enterprise Institute, was projecting a shortage of 900,000; by summer the National Education Association was saying that "as many as a million new public [school] teachers will be required by 1990"; a month later an article in the *New*

36

York Times was citing the figure of 1.3 million; and the year ended with the National Center for Educational Information citing shortages of 1.65 million. All these numbers were derived from the same set of projections by the then National Center for Education Statistics; more important, the words *shortage* and *replacement* were used interchangeably, and somewhat disingenuously. As a result, policy and decision makers were stampeded into mandating various remedies to affect the teaching force. Understandably, a parallel national study of teacher supply and demand, which reached a different conclusion, was ignored by those with a vested interest in seeing attention focused on improving teacher salaries and working conditions for teachers (Akin, 1984). Why policy makers ignored it is less certain. Why policy makers ignored the capacity of the nation's colleges and universities to replace those who were leaving the profession—the major source for the so-called shortage—was also unclear.

In any event, when *Time* magazine announced in its July 22, 1985, edition "And Now, a Teacher Shortage" (Bowen, 1985), it brought to the public's attention both the specter of a teacher shortage and the question of the quality of the beginning teacher pool. It legitimized the flurry of attention and served the vested interests. It changed the policy emphasis from increasing course requirements and intensifying pupil accountability to improving salaries and enhancing working conditions for teachers. It also called to the attention of many the absence of a system to forecast supply and demand of educational personnel at either the state level or on a national scale.

Teachers are drawn into teaching from multiple sources. Traditionally, a majority of beginning teachers are drawn from collegiate-based teacher education programs. A sizable number of beginning teachers, however, are arts and science graduates who gain provisional or probationary certification status. Another source of teachers is the "reserve pool" of individuals who are qualified to teach but currently are not teaching. The size of these three pools is the "supply side" of the labor market. In their initial efforts to affect the supply of teachers, policy makers sought to increase each of these pools. For instance, despite the absence of reliable and verified data regarding teacher shortages, policy makers responded to the reported shortages by enacting scholarship and loan programs to attract candidates to teaching. Such programs were implemented in virtually every state, with particular emphasis on recruiting mathematics and science teachers (American Association of Colleges for Teacher Education, 1985). As a second response, prompted in part by a shortage of teacher applicants, policy makers turned to alternative certification for teachers. New Jersey policy makers were the first to call for alternatives to the traditional undergraduate route through teacher education programs in universities and colleges. In New Jersey's program and similar programs in California, Arizona, and Delaware, attempts were made to reach a different audience than traditional collegiate students enrolled in education. These abbreviated training programs emphasized on-the-job learning in classrooms, with certain supports, in order to enlarge the candidate pool and to assure a flow of qualified persons into teaching. A third response has emerged in Connecticut, where emphasis has been placed on identifying individuals in the so-called "reserve pool" and encouraging them to enter teaching. This strategy, in combination with relatively high salaries to attract candidates from out of state, is another important policy intervention (Prowda and Grissmer, 1986).

It is still premature to make judgments regarding the impact these interventions will have on the supply of teachers throughout the country; indeed, the magnitude of the shortage is difficult to assess precisely, because frequent policy changes keep the situation in flux. These and other interventions, however, which have been growing in number each year, should serve as a rich area of policy research in the coming years.

Attempting to Forecast Supply and Demand
on a National Scale

By the third year of the reform effort, teacher leaders were announcing the existence of a national "crisis" in teaching and suggesting that a general shortage of teachers was imminent. Using projections based on a continuing decline of new teacher graduates and modest fluctuations in demand, Moore and Plisko (1985) concluded that by 1992 the supply would be only 65.6 percent of demand. That a more cautious route might have been followed was evident in the conclusions of college placement officers, who found subject and geographical shortages but no general shortage and did not project a shortage for the ensuing decade (Akin, 1984). At the same time, a number of state studies reinforced the message of prudence in projecting discrepancies in the availability of teachers and the need for teachers. Illinois, Delaware, and Washington were among those reporting no general shortages (Prowda and Grissmer, 1986), and a Rand Corporation researcher presented a policy memorandum that said, "We know almost nothing about how many teachers we will need, when, at what level, in which disciplinary fields, and in which parts of the nation" (Berryman, 1985).

It is difficult to understand why this disparity existed more than a dozen years after Senator Alan Cranston (D-California), in language added to the legislation reauthorizing the National Center for Education Statistics, mandated a collection of teacher supply and demand data. The dynamics that affect the teacher labor market are well understood. The relationship between teacher recruitment, teacher mobility, and teacher retention is detailed in numerous studies. Yet current research into labor market conditions for teachers in America points to a troubling state of affairs; indeed, the condition of current research is troubling. With disturbing regularity, last year's studies are cited in this year's studies, and "unpublished papers" typically cite three or four other "unpublished papers." Clearly, the inquiry into market conditions is moving at a very rapid pace. How this pace affects the accuracy of the information and the quality of public policy making is difficult to assess. What is certain is that this evolving inquiry does little to inform the "popular wisdom" of teacher market conditions.

Commonsense conceptions of market forces seem to be confirmed by the scholarly and quantitative conclusions of various analysts. Yet, in arriving at conclusions, these analysts sometimes overlook the need for specification and accuracy. They seem to assume that—in spite of problems with data col-

lection or experimental design—their conclusions are valid. This
assumption may be intrinsic to the nature of the teaching profession and its reliance on public policy decisions. Seeking to influence—indeed, to manipulate—data gathering to affect public
policy making is a fundamental characteristic of the enterprise
(Nelson, 1985). Given the magnitude of the investment in public elementary and secondary schools, now more than $140 bil-
lion, and the fact that teachers constitute the largest professional and technical work group in America, this interest is
understandable.

One problem that becomes apparent in a review of current studies is the lack of agreement on the assumptions, causes,
and policy implications of the current state of affairs. For example, in their estimates of teacher attrition, Darling-Hammond
(1984) uses a 9 percent figure, whereas Moore and Plisko
(1985) use 6 percent. Equally disturbing are the estimates of
the teacher reserve pool and its likely impact on the shortage
situation. In Maryland's study of teacher shortage, the concept
of a teacher reserve pool was excluded (see "Maryland Survey
Predicts Shortage of Teachers," 1985); in a Connecticut study,
on the other hand, reliance on the reserve pool was considered
(Governor's Commission . . . , 1985). Apparently, then, despite
all these efforts to study the teacher labor market, there is little
substantial understanding of what that labor market looks like,
what factors contribute to the current market conditions, and
what policy implications follow. As a result, the various conclusions lack consensus. To a large degree, this lack of consensus is
attributable to the incomplete formulation of research questions; is compounded by out-of-date, incomplete, or nonexistent data bases (for example, teacher benefits, teacher turn-
over, or teacher mobility); and is further complicated by
overextensions of the implications of the existing data. There is
little effort to aggregate the most reliable of existing data (that
gathered locally), and there has been almost no effort, to date,
to invest in longitudinal data concerning teacher careers. Nonetheless, data are often cited in the formulation of policies to
affect teachers and teaching.

Methodological Problems

Current research on the question of teacher supply and demand is concerned with a variety of related questions. First, is there a sufficient supply of teachers at present, and will there be a sufficient supply in the future? Second, what kinds of students choose teaching careers, and which of those who do choose teaching will stay in the profession for any length of time? Third, what qualities do we want in future teachers, and how do we develop them and ensure that they are there? These three questions are of paramount importance as one considers the nature of the school reform movement and the implications for teacher education programs on the nation's colleges and universities. Yet there appears to be little agreement about ways to address these questions.

The researchers who are currently studying these questions rely on different methodologies. There are a number of impediments to such investigations. Nevertheless, some recent studies have made significant contributions to the examination of the labor market. Among the most important is that advocated by Barro (1985), who urges that policy makers should think of supply and demand as functions instead of numbers that are tied to policy decisions. Persons seeking to influence either the supply or the demand side of the equation would concern themselves with enacting particular policies. Hawley's (1986) matrix of "Likely Effects on the Teaching Force of Selected Policies and Practices" offers a basis for such an approach. Response models would be developed to measure the reaction to changes in these variables.

Another promising example of recent investigations is found in Mark and Anderson's (1985) study of "survival rates." The authors examine the length of time teachers who enter in any particular year stay in the field. They then attempt to explain these survival rates in relation to public policies. For example, in examining their data, they find a decline in survival rates since the mid-1970s. They attribute this decline to the termination of young teachers as "school districts seek relief from financial pressures caused by budgets that do not keep up with inflation" (p. 419). A different tack is taken by Berry, Noblit, and Hare (1985), who conducted interviews at six universities and six school systems to investigate system recruitment patterns and characteristics sought in teachers (along with a number of other variables).

Each of these studies takes a different approach to the investigation of teacher labor market conditions. In most instances, triangulation of this sort is an effective test for the validity of experimental hypotheses and is a potential way to corroborate results. At first glance there seems to be little if any commonality among these articles from which to establish common definitions. While their investigations are substantially different, their insights allow for some interesting observations.

In their study of survival rates, Mark and Anderson (1985) found that career cycles had remained constant from the 1930s until the 1970s. In the early 1970s, survival rates peaked and have since returned to a more traditional level. The authors suggest that this peak resulted from an economic selection process whereby employment opportunities were scarce and school administrators were able to select candidates who would remain in teaching (p. 419). It is a sign of our limited understanding that Mark and Anderson are not able to elaborate on what factors determine that a candidate will remain in teaching. They suggest that the return to previously low retention levels is the result of the economic troubles of school systems. Younger teachers, they conclude, are fired both to cut immediate expenses and to head off the need for the salary increases that would accompany future advancement.

Berry, Noblit, and Hare (1985) sound a cautionary note and suggest that studies of the academic ability of the teacher supply pool are apt to mistake the basis of school systems' selection processes. According to these authors, administrators view teaching success as a function of the candidate's compassion, ability to work with students, and satisfaction with the system and community; and they place heavy emphasis on these characteristics in their hiring practices. Furthermore, these attributes are much more important than pecuniary rewards in determining the individual's chances of being hired and of remaining in the field.

Perhaps the most important line of recent research into teacher labor markets has been pursued by Philip Schlechty and Victor Vance. Their investigations of the relationship between academic ability and teacher selection and performance have been cited by reformers—for instance, the members of the Research and Policy Committee of the Committee for Economic Development (1985)—as the basis for their conclusions regarding a perceived decline in teacher quality and the need for a major new investment in American education. Indeed, a glance at the citations of subsequent studies suggests that a research paradigm may be taking shape around the work of these authors.

Vance and Schlechty's 1982 study seeks to validate and expand the results of their earlier examination of the relationship between academic ability and teaching career longevity. The 1982 study used as its sample the National Longitudinal Study of 1972 high school seniors who reported by 1979 that they had earned at least a bachelor's degree. These college graduates were divided into "recruits" and "nonrecruits" into education. Vance and Schlechty further divided the categories for purposes of comparing Scholastic Aptitude Test (SAT) scores between groups. By following the class through educational and career moves, Vance and Schlechty compared life choices toward and away from teaching with SAT scores. In this way they intended to show whether or not "academically able" students choose teaching careers and whether or not academically able teachers stay in the field. They concluded that "the teaching occupation disproportionately attracts and retains those with low measured academic ability and, conversely, disproportionately fails to attract or retain those with high measured academic ability" (1982, p. 24). This conclusion has subsequently served as the basis for numerous policy interventions and promoted sweeping changes in credentialing and educational requirements.

A number of considerations ought to be taken into account in interpreting Vance and Schlechty's results, especially if we are concerned with the formation of public policy. A principal concern of any such evaluation is the presence of coherent theory. To what degree does a research design arise from a coherent research agenda or follow from available data? In this sense, to what degree does it attempt to find a satisfactory answer to the underlying theoretical question? This question draws on the earlier mention of teacher selection processes; that is, the relations between measured academic ability, selection, and success. Vance and Schlechty sought a link between academic ability and survival rates. The SAT provided a potential measure of academic ability, and the 1972–1979 National Longitudinal Study allowed for an examination of educational and career patterns. As noted, Vance and Schlechty concluded that "effective teachers tend to be drawn disproportionately from among the most academically able of those who teach" (p. 25). However, the choice of a teaching career is a function both of a self-selection process and of an administrator selection process. As Berry, Noblit, and Hare (1985, p. 7) note, "School system officials reported they were not necessarily interested in prospective teachers with 'the best academic qualities.' They wanted those with 'a certain amount of intelligence,' but more importantly, they wanted the teachers to be able to 'relate to children and parents,' 'organize,' 'discipline,' 'withstand pressure,' and be involved in extracurricular activities. . . . Those who were 'very bright' were not necessarily what system officials needed or wanted."

The Schlechty and Vance studies led to a now commonly accepted way of assessing the quality of prospective teachers; namely, to analyze the annual reports of the College Board for prospective education majors. A disturbing note is that the members of the freshman college class of 1973 (who left college more than a decade ago) were given few of the aptitude and achievement tests that later classes were forced to take as a result of state mandates. Subsequent analyses of the same NLS data also indicated that three-quarters of the teacher group did not make a decision to enter teaching until after they were enrolled (Nelson, 1985). Also, and recalling Mark and Anderson's findings, the cohort entering teaching immediately prior to the group studied by Vance and Schlechty was notable for its high survival rate. This rate was higher than for any other cohort since the 1930s. These two factors suggest that, by the time the cohort in question reached the market, the prevalent oversupply of teacher candidates would have diverted many applicants to other fields. Furthermore, Mark and Anderson note that survival rates quickly returned to earlier low levels in the face of economic troubles. They speculate that new teachers were the hardest hit by this economic condition. All this suggests that the catalyst for career selection and longevity might be far different from that envisioned by Vance and Schlechty. Even these glimpses of context suggest that the cohort and time period in question may have been an aberration rather than representative of teacher labor pools and market conditions. These reservations suggest the need for a time-series analysis, perhaps using the next generation of NLS data to check for autocorrelation as a measure of the fluctuation of teacher supply and demand around equilibrium.

Another point of concern with the Vance and Schlechty research is its policy implications. As with the correspondence between SAT scores and teaching success, many of Vance and Schlechty's policy conclusions seem to take place purely at an intuitive level. For example, they discuss the negative impact of teacher salaries and make assumptions about the effect of salary adjustments. But they did not investigate the ratio of teaching salaries to salaries of other baccalaureate graduates over the years. Again, a time-series analysis seems called for. Analysis of this sort would help to measure the impact of salary on the attractiveness of the field.

Recent conceptual designs provide the first tentative formulations of the relevant research questions and operationalizations of the study of market conditions (Darling-Hammond and others, 1986). A major effort by the Rand Corporation to design a road map for studies of teacher characteristics, teacher supply and demand, and school policies should make a significant contribution. Sustaining that initiative and providing for wide dissemination of the results of the Rand studies are important to both policy makers and educators.

Supply of Teachers

For the past eighty years, there has been concern about finding and retaining an adequate supply of teachers. Each decade has produced numerous studies of the problem, with recommendations for remedying "shortages" and "surpluses" (Kluender, 1983). One unusual aspect of the decade of the 1970s was that, despite a surplus in numbers of beginning teachers and a significant decrease in elementary and secondary school enrollments, the number of teachers employed was constant. The educational mandates for bilingualism and handicapped education offset the reduced demand for teachers; thus, the size of the work force remained constant through the decade. As a result, the number of students enrolled in education in colleges and universities was seriously reduced.

The number of new teacher graduates declined from 317,000 in 1972 to 143,000 in 1982. More startling than this decline was the fact that the percentage of college graduates majoring in education decreased from 37 percent in 1971 to 17 percent in 1981; and a substantial number of these 1981 graduates could not find positions. This surplus stimulated a major decline of interest in teaching, as reflected in student preference surveys. College freshman interest in education majors and careers fell to a low of 6 percent in 1982 and 1983. Apparently, the oversupply of the previous decade plus the growing opportunities for women and minorities in other fields produced this downturn. In 1968, 38 percent of entering college freshmen women had indicated teaching as a career preference, as compared to 10 percent in 1983. The transition of teaching from a semicaptive market of talented women to a free market still dominated by substantial numbers of women has been one of the dominant themes of the past fifteen years.

Despite the awareness that substantial numbers of beginning teachers are drawn from various sources, a significant number of projections of "supply" are based on the concept of "graduates in education" (Raizen, 1986). While data on earned degrees fail to capture teachers who did not major in education, fail to identify minors in education (nine out of ten secondary candidates take their degrees in academic fields), and fail to consider emergency or provisional certificate holders and the growing number of persons who pass through alternative routes to certification, prediction of a shortfall is almost always based on past experience or trends in the production of new graduates in education. A parallel problem results when one ignores the states that traditionally "import" large numbers of beginning teachers from other states and offer projections based solely on their own graduates in education (Maryland, Georgia, and Florida, for instance, produce less than half of their beginning teachers).

Measuring the supply of beginning teachers, therefore, is difficult at best. Nonetheless, since each of our 1,222 teacher-preparing institutions has the capacity to increase productivity as market conditions change, we cannot continue to view "supply" as in decline. Widespread reports of enrollment increases in education, as well as actual increases in state issuance of certificates for beginning teachers, point to an upturn. Moreover, since all but two states are able to award emergency, substandard, or limited certificates, it is likely that school administrators and local school boards will always find persons to staff the classroom (Roth, 1986). The widespread use of "out-of-field" or misassigned teachers is also commonplace. Almost 200,000 teachers teach subjects for which they have had little or no preparation (Downing and Shanker, 1985), and more than 9 percent of beginning teachers are not certified in their principal field. Therefore, it seems far more appropriate to describe a shortfall of appropriately qualified candidates, rather than a shortage of teacher candidates.

Another theme of the past decade has been the alleged character of the teacher applicant pool. Almost all the state and national reports issued since 1983 describe the declining quality of the candidates in teacher education. As previously noted, SAT and ACT scores have been used to measure the academic ability of college-bound high school seniors planning to teach; a decline in these scores has become the principal means of determining a drop in the quality of beginning teachers. While these aptitude scores declined more sharply between 1973 and 1982 than for college-bound seniors as a whole, no one really knows whether any of the seniors who said that they planned to become teachers actually attended college, or were admitted into teacher education programs, or graduated, or were certified, or found teaching jobs. More accurate studies of candidate quality are needed—with agreement on what facets of quality should be examined and/or relate to performance in the classroom—before sound policy decisions can be made.

Nevertheless, policy makers have consistently relied on such reports and mandated a series of interventions designed to affect the flow of candidates into teaching. The most common of these efforts has been the introduction of testing programs for certification. Goertz, Ekstrom, and Coley (1984) found twenty-two states with testing programs for prospective teachers and another sixteen in the process of incorporating these efforts, consisting of a range of tests in basic skills as well as tests in particular content areas (although Florida, Georgia, and Virginia are assessing the performance of beginning teachers through observation). While disagreements persist regarding the predictive validity of such testing, there seems to be agreement that some sort of testing is appropriate prior to certification. What impact such testing will have on the number of beginning teachers remains uncertain.

A second way that policy makers have addressed the problem of perceived low quality is by changing credentialing and certification requirements. Although there have been changes in course requirements for prospective teachers, the most significant changes have been in the number of credits for field experiences and student teaching (Holmstrom, 1985). State-mandated prescriptions on the limits of pedagogical experiences are also growing in frequency, with some states (such as Colorado) abolishing undergraduate majors in education and other states (such as New Jersey) proposing to eliminate all undergraduate course work in education. The impact of such policies, particularly at a time of growing elementary school enrollments, may have unanticipated effects on the supply of new teachers. A parallel concern has to do with the widespread discussion of extended programs for teacher preparation (Lanier and others, 1986). Such programs require five or more years of college-based education before one is qualified to teach. When internship programs, supervised preservice training in special schools, are added to extended programs, teacher supply could be affected. As policy makers help to create such programs, they should consider the impact the programs will have on supply.

Sources of the Problem: Demand Size

In determining whether there is a "crisis" in the supply of teachers, one must analyze the need or demand for teachers. Demand is dependent on the growth in the school-age population and on state policies affecting pupil/teacher ratios, curriculum, and mandatory attendance. The interplay of these conditions over the next few years is expected to produce a relatively modest demand for additional teachers, with a small increase at the elementary level and a decline at the secondary level. Beyond 1990 it is more difficult to predict with certainty what will happen to demand.

Much of the current debate regarding shortage has focused on the growth issue and pointed to the "baby boomlet" of the 1980s and 1990s, when the children of the "baby boom" population (those born in the fifteen years following World War II) reach school. But the size of this boomlet is already known; and it will, in fact, represent only a bubble in the school-age population. It will return school enrollments to levels of the early 1970s, when some 51.3 million children were in school—with a rise from 44.3 million in 1984 to 49.8 million by 2000. For many this increase serves as the primary basis for projecting a shortfall in the number of teachers available to staff the nation's classrooms. What is not widely reported is that three-quarters of this population surge will be concentrated in only five states (California, Florida, Texas, Arizona, and North Carolina), and a majority of it will be minority (Hodgkinson, 1986).

A noteworthy aspect of this growth in numbers is the expansion and contraction of the system over the coming fifteen years. Elementary enrollments will rise from 30.9 million in 1985 to 35.4 million in 1993, for an increase of 14 percent. At the same time, secondary enrollments will continue to decline into the early 1990s, from 16.1 million in 1980 to 12.9 million in 1990 (a decrease of almost 20 percent), and then will slowly rise to 15.3 million in 2000. This shift in population will make it difficult to build and sustain a stable teacher work force and adds impetus to the efforts of some to fashion a cadre of "short-timers," instructors who serve for four to five years before moving to other careers. There is also some uncertainty about what will happen to the birthrate in the next twenty years. A few demographers suggest that the country will experience a new baby boom in the coming decade, while others reject this theory and point to a population decline. What is certain is that a declining fertility rate (the average number of children a woman has over a lifetime), now below the replacement level (the number of children one generation must have in order to replace itself with a generation of equal size), could produce a population decline. If it were not for the baby boom population and the large number of immigrants, the United States would already be headed toward an era of population decline. The impact this decline would have on schooling and the demand for school personnel is little understood at this time.

What is likely to produce a need for additional teachers is the loss of current teachers. The number of teachers between thirty-five and forty-four years old has increased from 20 percent in 1976–77 to 33 percent in 1983–84. The median age of the work force is now forty-one. As a result, the number of the current work force likely to retire has to be considered. Some estimate that as many as 900,000 of the current 2.3 million will quit or retire before 1995. The enactment of early-retirement programs can also have enormous impact on the demand side of the equation. In Michigan 18.2 percent of the work force became eligible for early retirement because of legislation enacted in 1985, thereby affecting in an extraordinary way the number of needed teachers. At the same time, there is uncertainty regarding economic conditions and the political consequences of "uncapping" mandatory-retirement policies. The influence of salaries and other incentives to hold current teachers needs critical examination.

An example of the uncertainty surrounding current policy and practice has to do with the introduction of performance or merit pay plans, career ladders, and differentiated staffing. Proponents of such structural changes for teaching believe that they will retain the most talented cadre of current teachers. What has happened calls for much more analysis: in those states that have introduced such schemes, there has been widespread dissatisfaction and some evidence of teachers leaving the profession. It remains unclear what impact these efforts will have in attracting more promising teachers to replace those who are leaving teaching. The introduction of national certification and the concept of professional practice boards to assure more promising candidates for teaching compound this problem. Whether such boards, controlled by teachers and their organizations, will be able to affect the flow of new teachers into the work force is an issue of enormous importance to policy makers. In their quest for professional status, teachers have argued for the right to set and administer admissions standards to the profession, just as professional boards in law and medicine set ethical standards, administer examinations, and award certificates. Conflicts between the desire for an adequate flow of qualified and competent beginning teachers (the public's interest) and the desire to restrict entry in order to effect changes in remuneration and working conditions (the profession's interest) will produce a tension between policy makers and teacher leaders. It is likely that such a tension will produce an even greater need for accurate supply-demand data.

In projecting changes in school staff needs, one has to consider the impact of the school reform movement and its call for raising standards and improving working conditions for teachers. Major investments in salaries for teachers are intended, in part, to attract and retain experienced and talented teachers. Whether such investments will have the desired impact (reducing the attrition rate and limiting the exit of good teachers) is uncertain. Similarly, changes in working conditions, the addition of specialists and support personnel, and reductions in class size could change the demand for new teachers. Reinforcing this demand could be new course requirements to meet the expectation of new core curricula, requiring, in turn, additional teachers to teach advanced sciences, foreign languages, and mathematics. All this suggests that the demand for new personnel to enlarge the work force is uncertain and will likely remain so for the coming decade. The uncertainty is compounded by the enormous size of the teacher work force (nearly the same as that of the nation's active-duty enlisted force and officer corps), the educational level of the present work force (more than 50 percent have an M.A. or an M.S. degree), and the subtle changes under way in the work force. The increased compensation for teachers (with salaries having risen more than 22 percent between 1982 and 1985 to an average salary of $23,546) is having an impact, but to what extent remains uncertain. It also remains difficult to predict what impact increased salaries will have on retaining more experienced teachers.

While almost half of all beginning teachers leave in the first seven years of teaching, recent research is showing that a surprising number of these teachers return at a later stage of their career (Harris and others, 1986). Those who leave teaching, plus the nearly 30 percent of the graduating teacher candidates who choose not to enter teaching, comprise the so-called "reserve pool"—a source of much speculation in this era of concern regarding shortage and surplus. The teacher reserve pool or reentry pool may consist of as many as 5 million persons (Graybeal, 1983), and we need to understand its characteristics and the incentives necessary to attract these persons back into teaching. While California and Connecticut have seen this pool as a ready source of talented teachers, other states have been less certain of the availability of these persons. Analysis of the pool is a research need.

Minority Teachers

Although we have described numerous uncertainties regarding the attempts to forecast a shortage of teachers, there is no doubt that the country is faced with a pervasive and overwhelming shortage of minority teachers. If one accepts the proposition that the work force should reflect the ethnic and racial characteristics of the larger society, then the number of minority teachers is significantly out of line with the society at large. At a time when minority enrollments in the public schools are increasing, the number of minority teachers is declining (Goertz, Ekstrom, and Coley, 1984). Some suggest that these numbers could be so out of proportion that the typical minority youngster could "meet" only two minority teachers out of the forty teachers whom he or she encounters in twelve years of schooling. Significant interventions to address this problem need to be in the forefront of every policy maker's agenda.

This is a problem of enormous proportions. It cannot be readily solved. The litany is now commonplace. *Education Week* highlighted the problem when it headlined its coverage "Black Teachers an Endangered Species" (Rodman, 1985). The number of black teachers in the work force has declined from 12 percent in 1970 to 8 percent by 1983—with a continuing decline to 5 percent expected by 1990. When this decline is juxtaposed with the rise in minority enrollments in our schools (up from 23 percent in 1970 to 27 percent in 1983 to an estimated 30 percent by 1990), the severity of the problem is highlighted. The need for more black teachers is self-evident (Baratz, 1986). The reasons for the decline are well known. The use of standardized test scores for entrance to and exit from teacher education programs, opportunities in other professional fields, the decline of minority participation in higher education, as well as the low quality of secondary schooling for minorities and the failure of blacks to participate in a college-bound curriculum contribute to this problem. Equally striking is the fact that only 48 percent of newly certified black baccalaureate recipients actually chose to teach (McBay, 1986). Efforts to address this problem must be mounted and sustained if minority participation in the wider society is to be assured. The impact of testing on the numbers of minorities available for careers in teaching—specifically, the incidence of failure on teacher tests for different ethnic groups—also needs to be better understood as one attempts to address this problem.

Conclusion

This chapter has argued that the widely discussed "crisis" of numbers may be more myth than reality. Enormous gaps in the available data make projections all but impossible. An emerging consensus seems to be that there are and will continue to be spot shortages in certain subject areas and in certain geographical regions. Definite shortages of minority teachers and teachers for urban schools can be predicted. It is not the lack of good intentions but the impossibility of aggregating enormous amounts of data for the more than 15,000 employing school districts that makes the task of assessing demand next to impossible. Many have concluded that perhaps the best we can do is to undertake local market studies and try to understand the dimensions of the problem by understanding these multiple studies. Others have concluded that we should shift the discussion from any attempt to use fixed numbers and instead focus on the effects of policies concerning teaching.

Of greater importance is an understanding of the reasons that have compelled national leaders to seize the concept of a national teacher shortage and to tie so much of the agenda for change to that concept. Having more competent teachers is in everyone's interest. Ensuring that the public allocates additional resources for teacher salaries and responds to the demands for better working conditions is essential. Whether the rhetoric of "crisis" will ultimately serve the interests of those who support the agenda will be evident in the coming years. If policy makers designate teaching as a profession and give teachers both more autonomy and more responsibility, as called for in recent reform reports, the problem of numbers should be ameliorated. If, on the other hand, they maintain their efforts for greater prescriptiveness, accountability, and bureaucratic control, then it is safe to predict that many current teachers will be driven out of teaching and many potential candidates will decide not to enter the teaching profession. In all their efforts, however, the policy makers need to act in an experimental mode because the issue of teacher supply and demand is one of enormous uncertainty.

Henrietta S. Schwartz

Attracting Better Students
to Teacher Education

According to current studies, our pool of teacher education candidates needs cleansing, broadening, and deepening. The brightest and the best students, at a time when our public schools—and indeed our nation—needs them, are not going into the classroom, and those who do get there either have trouble finding a job or leave after the first few years of teaching. The dropout rate among first-year teachers is about 50 percent. Moreover, new recruits to teaching are less academically qualified than those who are leaving. All is not lost, however. There is evidence that current education majors are as well qualified as noneducation majors are (Powell, Farrar, and Cohen, 1984). Nonetheless, by accepting less than the best and the brightest, universities and colleges are shortchanging the students in our nation's schools for the next twenty years. And then, in 2005, those poorly educated students will apply to our colleges and universities, and faculties will cry: "Oh, my, what unlearned applicants!" And who taught them? Furthermore: "The number of new entrants is insufficient to meet the coming demand for teachers. The most academically able recruits to teaching leave the profession within a very short time. Shortages of qualified teachers in subject areas such as mathematics and science are expected to grow over the next few years into a more generalized teacher shortage as enrollments increase and the supply of prospective teachers continues to shrink" (Darling-Hammond, 1984, p. iv).

Who is to blame? Some popular accounts suggest that potential teacher education candidates are competent, high-achieving liberal arts and science college students until they get into the professional programs in teacher education, where we give them a "dumb pill," put them through some methods courses, and send them out to the schools unable to cope. No individual and no institution can be that self-destructive. Clearly, the diminishing candidate pool is a reflection of a larger national problem, the decline in test scores over the last ten years. For example, SAT scores dropped from a mean of 453 in 1972 to 424 in 1980 and just began to show slight signs of recovery in 1985. In addition, according to Darling-Hammond (1984), academically talented women and minorities are choosing other occupations because both the pecuniary and the nonpecuniary rewards of teaching are unappealing. Teachers are increasingly viewed as bureaucratic functionaries rather than practicing professionals. Lack of input into professional decision making, restrictive bureaucratic controls, and inadequate administrative support contribute to this image and to teacher dissatisfaction.

Recent studies have claimed that the quality of teacher education programs and of certification criteria is highly variable (Feistritzer, 1984). Some states—New Jersey, California, and Texas—have even adopted alternative models that include no pedagogy or professional preparation but, instead, are based on on-the-job training as a route toward acquiring a teaching credential.

Teachers have always been asked to do more than teach the three R's. Ravitch (1983) traces the school's role in social reform over the last forty years and the attendant expansion of the teacher's role from transmitter of knowledge, skills, and mainstream beliefs and behaviors to social change agent. She contends that schools and teachers are not able to cure society's ills and should not have been expected to do so. "When they have failed, it was usually because their leaders and their public alike had forgotten their real limitations as well as their real strengths" (p. xii).

As if the above factors were not enough, schools are difficult places in which to work; they were built for children, with few accommodations for adults and adult interaction. Lortie (1975) talks about the isolation of the teacher and the lack of a career ladder; Kerr (1983) describes the bone-freezing boredom, because teaching, as it is presently structured, does not allow an adult to change functions or settings from time to time. Finally, Schwartz and colleagues (1983), Little (1981), and others look at the stressful working conditions found in urban schools and conclude that the system does not provide necessary rewards in status, security, and sociability. Teachers suffer from the "Rodney Dangerfield syndrome," in that they get little respect from a negative press and public, their jobs frequently put them in positions of fiscal and physical jeopardy, and they have little time or opportunity to make friends and interact with other adults during the course of the school day. From the perspective of intellectual stimulation, self-respect, economic security, and friendship, it would be irrational for the more able student to choose teaching as a career.

Now, what is the good news? What are the incentives to teaching as a career? Why did Mr. Chips and Miss Dove enter and stay in teaching? As one talks with teachers in the field and prospective teachers in training, it becomes clear that the perceived rewards are largely nonmaterialistic and reflect something of the missionary mythology surrounding teaching. For example, teachers mention their sense of having a mission in life, their pride in their profession, the joy of working with inventive young people, the satisfaction they experience when a child learns a lesson, and their belief that they are making a difference. They also speak of the opportunities to interact with their colleagues and with university people, the intellectual stimulation resulting from their need to be sure that they are current in their discipline, and the summers off for travel and professional development activities. Other rewards, in their view, are job security, the freedom to teach as they like once the classroom door is closed, and the sure knowledge that they are important and worthy participants in the society and carriers and transmitters of the skills, knowledge, beliefs, and behavior of the culture.

Prospective teachers speak of the ease of entry into the teaching ranks. They believe that teaching is good preparation for just about any other career and that only minimal retraining is needed after a maternity or military leave. They look forward to the short working days, which permit a woman to function in the traditional roles of wife and homemaker and allow the male teacher to take the administration courses related to advancement in the profession.

The contrasts embodied in the above paragraphs suggest that teacher education programs, as they socialize prospective teachers to the workplace, should not only present the good news but also prepare students for the bad; otherwise, expectations will be violated, and the *joie de vivre* that the beginning teacher brings to the school can quickly turn to resentment. Truth in advertising mandates that teacher preparation programs present a fair and accurate picture of the role and work environment for which the individual is being trained.

It seems that teacher educators are dealing with a number of dilemmas that must be addressed before we can begin to get specific about how to recruit the "best and the very brightest" into the ranks of teaching.

The Five Dilemmas

America is a multicultural nation featuring a core of mainstream beliefs and behaviors, which most cultures display and by which they are stereotyped—such as a common language or an accent or an attitude. That is, not all Los Angeles citizens speak English; in fact, more people speak Spanish in Los Angeles than in Acapulco. Not all Bostonians say "Hahvud" instead of Harvard. Not all Chicagoans are gangsters. Similarly, as Goodlad (1984) has pointed out in his massive *A Place Called School,* there is really no American public school system. Rather, there are some common starting points and some federal, state, and local regulations to which each school responds in a unique way. This is one of the problems any educational reform movement in this country faces: the time-honored tradition of local control of education. Because of the uniqueness of each state, municipality, and school, responses to reform initiatives can take an infinite variety of forms. The reform can proceed at very different rates in California and Florida and not move at all in some other areas of the country. The universal element in all these reforms is that they must in some way respond to five dilemmas before the renaissance can proceed.

This is an exciting time in American education and in teacher education. Major pieces of reform legislation in education have been passed and are now in the process of being implemented in forty-three states. Unless we attend to the five dilemmas, however, we shall have missed the opportunity generated by the many reports and the national attention focused on schools, teachers, and teacher preparation programs. Certainly, the brightest and best of our college students will want some responses to these dilemmas if we expect to recruit, retain, and induct them into teaching. The five dilemmas are described below.

Equity or Excellence. Most of the major reports issued concerning the state of education and teacher education have recommended raising entry standards for teaching and teacher preparation programs. Many states have individual exit examinations for credentialing purposes, and all have program approval mandates for teacher education programs. Historically, however, teaching has had relatively flexible admission and exit standards and has been the road to upward social and professional mobility for those who had been previously excluded from a share of the "goodies" of the mainstream society. Will higher standards exclude minorities, older adults, naturalized citizens, and others whose skills and talents are useful in schools but do not raise points on standardized tests? On the other hand, if standards are not raised, how will teaching and teacher education ever really achieve professional status and first-class citizenship in the professional and academic communities? Further, if teacher educators and the teaching corps miss the opportunity to elevate entry and exit criteria, and to upgrade schools and the intellectual caliber of those entering the profession, are they willing to be responsible for the next two decades of education and its consequences? Creative ways are called for to combine the principles of equity and produce excellent high-quality teacher education programs.

Egalitarianism Versus Differentiation: Career Ladders for Teachers. One of the core values of the teaching profession in public schools is: A teacher is a teacher is a teacher. That is, one teacher's opinion and contribution, in the formal structure of the school, is equal to any other's. Teacher associations and unions bargain for a single pay scale and for standardized hours for classes and preparation time; the only differences in salary are based on seniority. However, the reform legislation, researchers, and even one large union are calling for career ladders, differentiated rewards as a teacher displays special skills, knowledge, and initiative. Some legislation calls for mentor/ master teachers with more pay and greater responsibilities. Terrel Bell, the former Secretary of Education, has suggested that public school teachers adopt the university faculty ranking system. However, as one talks with individuals who have recently assumed the role of mentor/master, one hears that they deliberately downplay their new positions in working with their colleagues. It is evident that the egalitarian tradition is hard to overcome.

Teaching: Art or Science? This dilemma is a bit like the nature/nurture paradox. Are artists born or trained? Are teachers born or trained? Some would say that teaching is an instrumental or practical art, in that the acts in teaching are too complex to be reduced to a formula (Gage, 1978). Others (Berliner, 1984) maintain that over the last twenty years research findings have established a scientific, replicable, instructable basis for teaching as a science. One must learn the techniques and practice them before one can become a virtuoso in any art form. The same can be said for teaching. The problem is that we have not had a body of research containing validated, replicable, successful practices in teacher education programs or on teachers in training. Available information is based on research done with teachers in practice. We know what good teachers do. The question is: Can students be trained to do what good teachers do and be what good teachers are, or must some basic abilities be present before training?

The Curriculum: Standardization or Individualization?
Recent reports call for more standardization in the content of
the curriculum at the K-12 level as well as for the teacher preparation programs. One report suggests that the "mess" in teacher credentialing standards across the states in content areas
could be resolved if a national teachers' examination in content
fields were required for certification (Feistritzer, 1983). Such a
requirement strikes at the heart of the academy's tradition of
academic freedom, at the right of professors to teach without
restraints, to develop curriculum, and to structure the delivery
as they wish within peer-determined limits. Credentialing of and
legislative mandates about teacher preparation programs reduce
that autonomy and enhance standardization. In the role of pro-
tector of the commonweal, state agencies will continue to move
toward standardization of curriculum and teacher preparation;
and in the name of academic freedom, university faculty and
public school teachers will resist.

Focus of Instruction: Curriculum or Child? Given the
limited amount of time most programs use to prepare a teacher,
choices must be made about the focus of the preparation en-
deavors. In the classroom does one teach the curriculum or the
child? The answer to that question may specify the institutional
strategy to be emphasized. Will it be mastery learning, small-
group instruction, large-group activity, coaching, time-on-task
strategies, classroom discipline, working with alterable variables
or the double sigma effects, homogeneous grouping, hetero-
geneous grouping, audiovisual and computer aids? Shall the
handicapped be mainstreamed into regular classes or placed in
special instructional units? At the university level, the content
of the curriculum seems to take precedence over the student as
an individual. In the kindergarten class, the reverse is true. How
do teachers strike a balance, and what happens if they do not
accommodate both foci?

Approaches to Solutions. The five dilemmas are not in-
soluble. They can be managed, even resolved, with sufficient
valid research. Innovation and creative practices can reconcile
the seeming paradoxes with a "both/and" approach. Some accommodations can be made wthout sacrifices of quality. The

resolution of the dilemmas must be attempted with respect for different views, with appreciation for the cultural diversity of the public school population, and with considerable awe for the tremendous cultural ballast of the school as an institution. This last should not be overlooked. The schools have maintained their purpose and relationship with culture for the last two thousand years, since the days of Socrates. Above all, the dilemmas must be approached with the understanding and admiration for the crucial nature and centrality of the role of the teacher in any reform movement. The training and occupational socialization offered by any teacher preparation program can only be as good as the faculty, the processes, and the candidates incorporated into the system.

A Conceptual Structure

There are three assumptions basic to the following discussion: first, that teaching is an instrumental art, the preparation for which can be based on a core of scientific research findings; second, that the act of teaching is practiced in schools, which are social systems composed of institutional roles defined by expectations and filled by individuals with unique personality needs; third, that the goal of any educational institution is to produce competent, intelligent, skilled, and productive persons. Given these assumptions, what sort of model would best describe ways to attract the best and the brightest to the field?

Probably the most efficient and effective model would be one that describes, analyzes, and predicts a variety of person-preparation-performance fits. There is a reasonably solid body of research-engendered information about the kinds of people who make good teachers and about the teaching techniques that have proved effective. These findings could be used to develop a series of selection models, one for rural education settings, one for secondary education, another for early childhood education, and still another for vocational education. Teacher preparation programs, using the findings from effective teaching research, could develop a series of training modules for each setting or grade level, matched with a projection of who would best fit

each setting. After the generic core, some students would prepare for rural settings, some for specific programs in urban education, some for early childhood, and others for teaching history
or music or vocational education. Then a supervised internship
and induction period of two to three years would ease the transition from student to teacher and reduce the excessively high
dropout rate among beginning teachers. In this system rewards
would be commensurate with expertise.

Many scholars have indicated that systematic and specific
teacher education programs are now possible, based on past and
ongoing research on the peculiar nature of the teacher's work.
The college or university from which the teacher graduated and
the school where the teacher is placed would collaborate on ongoing in-service training, thus reducing the false dichotomy between preservice and in-service training. One of the elements of
any profession is that initial preparation and continuing training
are part of the same longitudinal career commitment. In effect,
these are the recruitment, selection, training, and induction processes used by medicine and law, and they represent a traditional model of socialization into a profession.

It is at this juncture that the teacher education socialization model breaks down. Recruitment, selection, training, and
induction into other professions ensure the individual of certain
benefits, which are not currently present in teaching. One of the
norms of any profession is that the professional enjoys some
form of public and private client trust, and this trust allows peer
evaluation and sanction. The professional is expected to obey
an ethical code emphasizing service and will make a commitment to best practices. The training period is long. Entry is difficult. Career rewards and the good life are predictable and are
based on enhanced skill and knowledge, hard work, and excellence in professional performance. Teaching, as it is currently
structured, does not meet these criteria. In order for teaching to
qualify as a profession, a number of things would have to happen: higher salaries, subsidized professional training and internship programs, individual career ladders, a synthesized body of
teaching knowledge for the novice, continuous on-the-job professional development, and teaching as a year-round position.

There are indications that some progress is being made toward achieving professional status as a by-product of the reforms being called for in teaching, schools, and preparation programs. California has mandated that a beginning teacher's salary be $18,000; experiments are under way to add those difficult beginning years of teaching to the initial preparatory period and to substantially lengthen the period of teacher training, enabling newcomers and experienced teachers to collaborate as colleagues in school improvement (Bush, 1983; California Commission on the Teaching Profession, 1985).

At this time it is difficult to develop a holistic model of recruitment, retention, and induction for an occupation that is still undergoing an "identity crisis." Questions about the recruitment and retention of traditionally underrepresented minorities in teaching might have better answers if candidates knew whether they were seeking a lifelong commitment or a preliminary occupational activity, as an entry to another work role. Although there are certain commonalities in any model designed to address problems of attrition, selection, and retention, we still need to know what motivates a student's choice of preparatory programs.

Despite impediments that current evidence suggests—that most college-bound high school students are not interested in teaching as a profession (Mangieri and Kemper, 1984)—are there ways to recruit, select, retain, and graduate competent students? Of course there are, but with one final caveat, as expressed by Tinto (1982, p. 699) in his comprehensive work on student attrition: "However constructed or designed, no program to reduce attrition is better than its implementation and management within the institution. . . . It is one thing to conceive of, even design, an institutional retention effort; it is another to implement and manage one within the often rigid maze of institutional structures." If you read "system of recruitment, selection, retention, and induction" for "program to reduce attrition," then you have the basic principle for any comprehensive effort to attract talented students to teacher education.

In summary, a comprehensive conceptual model for recruitment and retention in teacher education and in the field of teaching today would necessarily be incomplete because the field is in a crucial transition period. Thirty years ago one could say with some certainty: (1) Recruit women and minorities, for they will stay in the field. There are bright students among these groups who view teaching as a career on the road to upward mobility. (2) Select academically well-qualified students who are nurturing, like to work with children, are not concerned with working conditions too much, love their subject, and want to stay close to home. (3) Retain and induct into the profession those students who perform well academically and serve a short supervised student-teaching hitch; then cut them loose after graduation to sink or swim. Today we cannot count on these principles; for the world has changed, and so have we.

Recommendations for Action

What initiatives can universities, teachers, and public agencies pursue to attract competent students to teacher education? The following recommendations are predicated on the notion that teaching is a profession for some, and for others an entry-level first occupation leading to diverse professional careers. The research suggests that these two strands are sex specific, but the recommendations apply for all groups, although there are special recommendations related to underrepresented minorities. The main starting point for any teacher preparation program must be a comprehensive knowledge base in the liberal arts and sciences.

From my perspective, *recruitment* of particular populations implies that *selection* models and criteria have been defined and applied to the applicants. *Retention* means not just reducing dropouts from the university but reducing the shocking attrition rates for beginning teachers. Supervised induction to teaching must be part of any retention plan. Graduation from the university in this view simply marks a different state of professional preparation for teaching. There is much to be done about schools as workplaces, salaries, status, credentialing, and the like; and teacher educators in the university and in the schools can influence decisions in these areas. I am reminded of what Margaret Mead said when she was asked how one begins to educate children for world peace. "The answer is everywhere at once." The recommendations begin everywhere at once.

Planning

1. Any comprehensive, longitudinal recruitment and selection plan for attracting students into teacher education must include both a broad base and a locally targeted public relations element, alternative models of desirable candidates, an examination of criteria and procedures for admission of students to programs, provisions for redesigning the curriculum where appropriate, and provisions for retraining faculty and articulating with K-12 schools, community colleges, and other agencies with potential candidates.

This generic recommendation lists some of the essential elements of an institutional effort to attract well-qualified candidates to teaching, including underrepresented minority students, such as Hispanics. The examination of admissions criteria could result in higher standards and, at the same time, expanded remedial services to students who need academic work but have the motivation and other characteristics deemed desirable from the selection models developed. Provisions should also be made to accommodate the atypical candidate who may not fit the model as snugly as others.

Implementation

2. The university should create cadres of trained recruiters (composed of faculty in teacher education and the arts and sciences, media experts and market research strategists, and liaisons to target populations), who should contact local groups in order to build community support and gain access to potential candidates.

Business and industry, the military, and the government spend millions of dollars to entice the best and the brightest into the fields that service their enterprises. Available technology would allow a university and a teacher education program to follow those examples: to target a potential population, saturate the media and the school or community college, engage in active recruiting, and begin to build some bridges to the programs. Time, resources, and the willingness to use commercial techniques to attract students to teacher education are needed for this type of approach. A five-year trial period is recommended before any summative evaluation of the effectiveness of the effort is done and decisions are made about continuation of the effort.

3. Teacher educators and university recruiters should participate in regional, local, and national events to share recruitment strategies, learn from others, and form networks so that students can move from one educational agency to another with a minimum of anxiety.

Personal contacts among counselors, admissions officers, and teacher educators should be encouraged. Too often transfer students from community colleges or secondary schools experience a sometimes debilitating culture shock upon entry to the university. Research indicates that the retention rate is higher when counselors and admissions officers know each other and can work together. The same concept can be applied to entry into the teacher education program. When a faculty member from an arts and science department personally refers a student to a faculty member in the school or department of education, the student is given a sense of security and self-esteem. The implementation of this recommendation is relatively low in cost, but it does involve institutional commitment to the time as well as travel funds necessary to support networking activities. It may also mean endorsing university-wide teacher education committees and exchanges to connect the rest of the university to the teacher preparation programs.

4. Universities and teacher preparation programs should employ and train skilled counselors to work with their counterparts at two- and four-year institutions that have large numbers of underrepresented minority students.

Attention should be given to the role-modeling aspect of this endeavor; and, whenever possible, the counselors themselves should be members of underrepresented minority groups.

A similar group in teacher preparation programs should be available to guide all students through the maze and mysteries of the certification processes, and to provide academic and some personal counseling if necessary.

5. Any recruitment officer in teacher education must adhere scrupulously to the principle of "truth in advertising" when advising students about the career of teaching.

This recommendation costs very little money, but it does require a great deal of self-analysis and occupational analysis. Interested students might be directed to talk with recent graduates or students currently in training, to visit several schools, or to recontact their favorite teacher. Career options must be presented to teacher education students; otherwise, their unfulfilled expectations will continue to result in abnormally high attrition rates during the induction period.

6. A variety of collaborative models and experimental programs are available for replication and should be considered, particularly at the middle and high school levels.

When schools and universities actively collaborate on teacher training programs, additional benefits accrue. High school students can become acquainted with university professors, and high school teachers can identify potential candidates for the teaching profession. Some programs have established tracking systems for talented students, who are invited to campus during the summer to participate in tutoring or preprofessional activities. Socialization to the profession should start early, and these "learning bridge" programs seem to be very successful experiments.

7. The university and the teacher education program should examine their selection and entry criteria for equity violations and determine whether sufficient remediation opportunities exist to accommodate underrepresented minority populations.

California, among other states, now has an entry examination for all candidates in teacher education. This examination also serves as an exit criterion, for one cannot earn a credential unless he or she passes the California Basic Educational Skills Test (CBEST). This test, like most others, has a verbal, a mathematics, and a writing component. After two years the statewide test results indicated that fewer Hispanic students passed the examination, particularly the language portion, than other students did. In such instances the academy (the whole academy, not just the teacher preparation programs or the schools and colleges of education) must take responsibility for remediating the deficiencies in language skills. Equity and excellence can be accommodated with planning, resources, and commitment. To lower standards is patronization; to prepare students to meet standards is good judgment.

8. Financial aid information must be made available by the university and teacher education programs to students before and during their course of study in a professional preparation program. If the teacher preparation period is extended, then increases in financial aid are necessary.

9. In addition to the recommended actions at the university, teacher educators should work with the public, the legislators, and their colleagues in the field to design and implement appropriate career ladders and role differentiation in the schools. Teachers should be encouraged to assume responsibility for their own profession by controlling entry, by evaluating their colleagues, and by working for increased status for the profession.

10. Teacher educators and the profession must enlist public and administrative support to redesign the schools as workplaces, to make teaching a full-time job, and to restructure schools as places where adults as well as children can learn and develop.

Research and Development

11. Additional work must be done on the person-preparation-practice syndrome in order to fine-tune the system of selection and training of teachers.

Research studies should be mounted to follow up some of the work on teacher stress and burnout, which has revealed that what is creative tension to one teacher in an urban school is unbearable stress to another. What are the coping strategies, personality characteristics, family background, and teaching techniques exhibited by individuals in various settings? These data have implications for recruitment and selection as well as for training and entry into teaching.

12. Various models of recruitment, selection, retention, and induction should be mounted in experimental modes.

Several diverse institutions should be given appropriate funding to mount programs, with the understanding that there will be extensive documentation to determine which programs are most effective in recruiting the brightest and the best and in keeping them in the profession at least five years. Experimentation with the Master of Arts in Teaching format, followed by a supervised internship for the first three years, is recommended by Robert Bush (1983), B. O. Smith (1983), and many other scholars. If these support systems are promised during training, the attractiveness of the profession might be enhanced.

Finally, the university and teacher preparation programs must look to themselves and engage in program revision and faculty development, as well as maintaining connections with research and the field. The best recruitment, selection, and retention programs will go for naught if the core of the professional preparation program is not concept and research based, content rich, intellectually stimulating, practically useful, and generative of pride in the graduate. So where do we begin to clear, expand, and deepen our pool? Everywhere at once, my friends, everywhere at once!

6   *Edward R. Ducharme*

Developing Existing
Education Faculty

If teacher education programs are to change significantly, and
they must change if they are to survive, they will do so through
the efforts of existing teacher education faculty. The plethora
of national reports calling for improvement in the lower schools
has led to calls for reform in teacher preparation programs. Ad-
vocacy for a postbachelor's program for teacher preparation is
growing; demands for quality scholarship and research in education are increasing; standards for recruitment and acceptance
of applicants into teacher preparation programs are rising; and
resources are at their usual low ebb. These conditions must be
met by a largely in-place teacher education faculty, a faculty
prepared with one set of assumptions, confronted during their
careers with changing emphases, and facing a future filled with
change. There are thus both institutional and personal reasons
for faculty development efforts.

   Interest in faculty development across all departmental
lines has increased dramatically—as demonstrated by Sanford's
(1980) *Learning After College,* Freedman's (1973, 1979) *Facilitating Faculty Development* and *Academic Culture and Faculty
Development,* Gaff's (1975) *Toward Faculty Renewal,* and other works. The changing nature of higher education institutions,
the aging of the faculty, the shifts in age cohorts in the student

body, the growth of knowledge in disciplines, calls for institutional reforms, changing economic situations, and advances in instructional strategies—these and other conditions contribute to the need for faculty development.

This chapter will focus on the developmental needs of teacher education faculty, describe contexts for their development, provide background on adult development, and urge strong leadership in promoting teacher education faculty development by institutional leaders, particularly at the executive level.

Traditional Faculty Development

Traditional faculty development has historically been limited to improvement in instructional and research capacities. "The literature that has developed deals mostly with meeting instructional and scholarly needs, little with perspectives from adult development, which might highlight personal as well as professional faculty needs" (Ducharme, 1981, p. 30). Boice (1984, p. 196) makes a similar point: "Faculty developers rarely go beyond instructional development, despite calls for broader programs of organization and personal development. . . . Examples of faculty improvement are almost entirely limited to teaching skills—whereas evidence for development of personal qualities such as 'inner directedness' . . . is even rarer and, apparently, less influential." The demands of the multifaceted world and the increased knowledge of adult development require that faculty development efforts expand beyond improved pedagogy and scholarship. There is nothing inherently wrong in conventional faculty development approaches; they are simply inadequate for the range of faculty in today's institutions.

Most institutions provide opportunities for faculty development: conferences, workshops, grants programs, travel, and sabbaticals. Participation is often dependent on the degree to which the organization as well as the individual will profit. The sabbatical is the most visible and valued of institutional development activities; it may also be the most tradition bound. For some the sabbatical is a fulfilling experience; for others it is a frustrating one as presently practiced in many colleges and universities. The sabbatical is often awarded as a result of the individual's compliance with rigorous institutional criteria. The University of Vermont's statement in its *Officers' Handbook* is a typical example: "The objectives . . . are to promote the professional development of the individual faculty member and to enhance the educational environment of the university. . . . Award of a sabbatical leave is based on the expectation that the officer will utilize the period of the leave to add to knowledge in the academic field, to enhance teaching effectiveness, to broaden fields of competency, or to acquire other valuable professional experience. Appropriate means of achieving these aims include sponsored or unsponsored research, formal or informal study, creative activity appropriate to the individual's responsibility within the university" (University of Vermont, 1984, sec. 200-235). Words and phrases such as *professional, add to knowledge, broaden fields of competency* direct faculty into strictly academic areas of inquiry, with traditional criteria to be applied to both the award of the sabbatical and to the evaluation of the work following completion.

These traditional norms for sabbaticals may well fit the plans and needs of most faculty; but broader guidelines are necessary for faculty in professional schools, with the ongoing changes in their professional spheres of work, the emerging needs of their students, and their own developmental states. In the University of Vermont statement, the words *informal study* and *creative activity* are possible points of entry into more imaginative sabbaticals, ones more closely tied to faculty personal as well as professional development.

Colleges and universities contribute to the singular scope and purpose of faculty by rewarding most those who most closely follow traditional rites and rituals. Junior faculty emulate senior faculty who have succeeded because of rigorously following early delineated goals. Whatever thought and energy go into faculty development at many institutions are directed at providing research and rest opportunities (sabbaticals), so that faculty can do even better what they have been doing. Development thus means fulfillment of one's early promises and goals.

While these traditional views and practices may meet the goals of some teacher education faculty, the need for a larger vision of faculty development is requisite if they are to meet their professional responsibilities with a sense of renewal and commitment. Some understanding and appreciation of adult development principles are necessary for leaders in higher education to promote faculty development.

Issues in Adult Development

As observed earlier, the traditional goals for faculty development have been instructional improvement and scholarly research, activities not necessarily including any consideration of an individual's developmental level. Leaders interested in more than teaching and research when they consider faculty development will find the literature on adult development of interest. Obviously, a chapter such as this cannot provide a full review of the adult development literature and its implications. However, some information and background are appropriate.

Adult development has become a legitimate field of inquiry within the past several decades. Major figures include Erikson (1950), Harvey, Hunt, and Schroeder (1961), Kohlberg (1969), Levinson (1977), Loevinger (1976), and Neugarten (1968). In general, developmentalists have studied life from youth through old age and elicited trends and themes about human existence. All see humans passing through age or stage changes that affect how they act and react in particular settings, what their interests are and might become, where they seek fulfillment. Some see life composed of cycles that individuals pass through; others see life as a series of roles or tasks. Common to almost all developmentalists is the idea that most human beings living in a particular place and time are likely to undergo common growth and development experiences, albeit at perhaps slightly different times in their lives. Life's tasks and stages are more stressful for some than others.

Summarizing the views of a number of developmentalists, Knox (1977, pp. 49-50) observes: "Young adulthood is considered to have an early stage between eighteen and twenty-five and a late stage between twenty-six and thirty-nine. Middle age is considered to have an early stage between forty and fifty-five and a late stage between fifty-six and sixty-four. Old age is perceived [to have] an early stage between sixty-five and eighty and a late stage between eighty-one and death. . . . The stereotypes that people hold of adults reflect a shift from perceiving late adolescents and early young adults as active, energetic, and outgoing; to perceiving middle-aged adults as understanding, mature, restrained, and controlled; to perceiving the old and aged as energyless, inactive, socially inefficient, and mystical."

Charlotte Bühler found adults between the ages of eighteen and twenty-five dominated by the issue of occupation and life dreams. For the next twenty years, from twenty-five to forty-five, the adult is concerned with "creative expansion" and the realization of possibilities in regard to occupation, marriage, and home. The years from forty-five to sixty-five are characterized by the "establishment of inner order," with a reassessment of priorities (Glickman, 1985, p. 47).

One can draw several conclusions from these general statements: No one theory of adult development sheds light on all human beings, but knowledge of many theories leads to broader understanding; most people manifest a variety of developmental persona in different situations, and one should be wary of drawing conclusions from limited exchanges with individuals and attempting to prescribe programs, remedies, enrichments, incentives, punishments, and other possibilities based on such exchanges. Further, certain activities and interests may be more appropriate for and better accomplished by adults at different periods in their lives. For example, concentrated study of one aspect of scholarly work may fit an individual at a particular time while a radically different and new emphasis may be appropriate at another time. Developmental activities in higher education should be flexible enough to accommodate these different aspects of individual lives.

It was once commonly believed that development stops at a certain age, that patterns set during youth and young adulthood are essentially unchangeable. As people grow older, according to the traditional view, it becomes harder to do new things, and change becomes more difficult. Sprinthall and Thies-Sprinthall (1983, p. 22), among others, refute this notion: "Adults do not regress cognitively, and it may be possible to restart the developmental motor, so to speak, to nurture further growth."

The majority of current teacher education faculty are in the forty-plus age cohort—a condition that would, if one follows the old beliefs about unchanging adults, suggest little likely change in their behavior. Yet the opposite may be true, for the work of Sprinthall and Thies-Sprinthall and others suggests that people do not lose the potential for growth and development as they age. This statement calls into question another commonly held belief: that people stop developing or are hindered from developing once they attain certain roles. That is, they often behave or are expected to behave according to norms seen as appropriate to the role; therefore, they reach developmental plateaus. Both beliefs are harmful to institutions and individuals: to institutions, because they are deprived of contributions faculty might make; to individuals, because they often become rigidified in place.

Knowledge of adult development enables one to cast off stereotypical views of others and of oneself; to understand that faculty appearing to be in similar positions in life are actually feeling and thinking quite differently; to accept that what works for one group of faculty may be very inappropriate for another group.

Needs and Characteristics of Teacher Education Faculty

For many the traditional possibilities for faculty development have worked quite well, perhaps for some more than others. But the concept of faculty development must include more than the single-minded pursuit of inquiry in one field. It must acknowledge the increased knowledge about adult development. Further, those in positions of influence must argue that teacher education faculty require broader concepts of faculty development than those held for faculty in some other disciplines.

Teacher education faculty prepare teachers to recognize

and respect the many dimensions of their own students and clients, dimensions that extend beyond where they work and how productive they are. According to McNergney and Carrier (1981, p. 18), teacher educators also should take into account the development of those with whom they work: "In the course of teaching and learning each day, a teacher changes, but not always in a positive direction. If the teacher educator were to attend only to the present, ignoring the teacher's history over the course of the year (or years), the prospects for teacher growth would be greatly diminished. For this reason, teacher development should encourage people to view changes in teacher behavior as points on a continuum rather than as isolated events." One can see the implications of this statement by substituting *faculty member* for *teacher* and *president or vice president* for *teacher educator* in the passage. How ironic that teacher education faculty frequently inhabit work environments where only their work merits consideration but where they themselves, in teaching and working with others, must take into account many personal variables.

Data collected on over 1,000 professors of education (Ducharme and Agne, 1982) indicate that approximately 45 percent are between the ages of forty-one and fifty, and that 65 percent have been in the same institution for more than six years, 41 percent more than eleven years. Regardless of their particular views on how humans develop and what the key issues are, most developmentalists would agree that people in this age cohort have dealt with the early commitments of adult life to work, family, and self; have survived some period of reassessment—generally in the thirties—of these earlier commitments; and have now reached a period of midlife transition. They are beginning to see the finite nature of their own lives and careers. Those with patterns of previous success may want to pursue what they have been doing; but others with similar successes may be willing to experiment, to try new things. Many no longer feel the threats of failure because they have known success and believe that they can be successful in other things. Often people in this age cohort are becoming more tranquil about life; they may seek closer personal relationships. The earlier needs to be constantly competitive may have ebbed sharply. These and other issues should guide the thinking and planning of the development of teacher education faculty. Many teacher education faculty may be ready for new direction in their careers, prepared to assume leadership roles; they may be ideal candidates to lead and promote change and reform efforts. They may require only effective leadership, strong development, and potent support.

Development is difficult in constrained and predictable environments. Teacher education faculty have spent most of their lives in constraining places, their roles defined for them to a considerable degree, with few opportunities to express new or divergent views. This is true for faculty in the traditional roles in arts and science departments but even more so for teacher education faculty, who must accommodate to the behavior norms of the traditional higher education faculty and also remain sensitive to their public constituents; namely, teachers and administrators in the lower schools. They also face, on many campuses, the suspicion of other faculty about their campus role, the legitimacy of their work, the quality of their students, and the intellectual rigor of their programs.

Further, many education faculty began their careers in the lower schools, where they may have acquired habits that define or limit their own institutional behaviors. Life in the lower schools is even more constrained than life in higher education, as the Carnegie Task Force on Teaching as a Profession (1986, p. 39) describes: "Teachers work in an environment suffused with bureaucracy. Rules made by others govern their behavior at every turn. Perceptive researchers have told us for years that teachers are treated as if they have no expertise worth having. . . . Decisions made by curriculum supervisors, teacher training experts, outside consultants, and authors of teachers' guides determine how a teacher is to teach." The environment described is hardly one to promote independent, autonomous behavior. As has been observed (Ducharme and Agne, 1982; Lanier and Little, 1985), the lower schools are the points of professional origin of more than three-quarters of education faculty. Thus, teacher education faculty have spent their lives, generally speaking, in *two* constraining environments: the public schools and higher education.

Challenges to Existing Faculty: Curriculum and Students

Teacher education faculty face two challenges: to attract highly qualified candidates and to provide a rigorous curriculum to prepare them as highly qualified, autonomous, analytical teachers, capable of carrying out the reforms that are critically needed in the lower schools. Both of these challenges are vital to faculty development, since high-quality students and a high-quality program foster faculty growth.

There has been long-standing concern about the ability of teacher education to attract and retain highly qualified candidates. Lanier and Little (1985) observe that schools of education have traditionally attracted their share of upper-ability students and more than their share of lower-ability students; what they become known for, however, are their alleged low-quality students. The National Commission for Excellence in Teacher Education (1985) found conflicting evidence about the quality of teacher education candidates but also noted that demographic and social factors will make it even harder for institutions to recruit able teacher education students in the future (pp. 5-6).

Vital questions facing many institutions, whether they provide four-year preparation programs or fifth- and sixth-year programs, are: How can we retain the few highly qualified candidates initially entering preparation programs? How can we dramatically improve the preparation of the less able? How can we discourage the bottom 10 to 15 percent, who, once in, persist in teaching careers longer than any other group? A partial answer to the three questions is: by developing a rigorous, intellectually respectable, professionally useful, and pedagogically potent program for all preservice candidates.

A curriculum more rigorously and artfully crafted will attract candidates who possess the characteristics that, according to Heck and Williams (1984, p. 42), influential teachers possess: "optimism about the future; authenticity; concern; belief and trust in human potential; enthusiasm; confidence; high ethical standards; willingness to admit errors; a sense of spontaneity and emotional involvement; and an innate desire to achieve." If schools of education communicate their belief that the curriculum matters, that individuals must undergo rigorous training prior to becoming teachers, that there is shared knowledge and experience, able students might be attracted to the teaching profession. Perhaps Dreeden's (1970) lament of more than a decade ago would be reversed: "Schools of education, then, mobilize few of the resources apparently necessary to form an organizational community among teachers. They do not subject students to the intense pressures and crises that contribute to the creation of solidarity around them, a solidarity that can produce unanticipated benefits in occupational learning" (p. 42).

Mature faculty would gain strength and power from a curriculum of demonstrable worth and merit. The age cohorts of teacher education faculty demonstrate that the next decade is the time of summing up for many, of wanting to feel pride in past accomplishments, of leaving a legacy of worth. And, indeed, a legacy of worth is a consideration of merit to teacher education faculty, who presently constitute at least 60 percent of those who will be teaching in professional education programs in the year 2000 (Ducharme and Agne, 1982).

One curriculum area in need of development is that of the knowledge and understanding of research in learning and teaching. More quality research in education is evident each year. "Recent and numerous advances in pedagogical knowledge can now, for the first time, be used to provide education with a scientific foundation. What we need now is a great reform in teacher education" (Berliner, 1985, p. 4). The reform advocated by Berliner and others is dependent upon more effective dissemination and utilization of current and future research findings.

The incorporation of research into teacher education programs will not happen, however, unless the diverse nature of teacher education faculty is taken into account. The work of teacher educators is exceedingly complex:

Teacher educators appear to be caught between two conflicting worlds. The first is the old world, caricatured by people who had, by whatever process that seemed appropriate, been judged effective and gone on to university studies to acquire a doctorate or, equally often, been hired out of the public schools by a local college or university to work with undergraduates. Long on experience and sure of their views, these individuals taught and continue to teach their students using their own past as their source of pedagogy. The new world is caricatured by more recently appointed faculty, who are likely to have undergone more rigorous graduate work, more inclined to believe in research, disposed to teach from a set of beliefs or principles anchored in some research. Some would argue that the first set of individuals continue to do the major bulk of the teaching while the second group assume the research function or burden [Ducharme, 1986, p. 56].

In the late 1980s and the 1990s, the composition of teacher education faculty will slowly but steadily change as retirements occur and enrollments increase moderately. Newly prepared faculty entering the professoriate have been prepared differently from those they are replacing, since the research emphasis in doctoral institutions has increased dramatically in the last decade. It is now common to be able to hire beginning faculty who have published scholarly work. They have already been inculcated into the scholarly ethos of higher education. Despite their skills in scholarship and research, however, new faculty must also be inducted into the working professoriate, with its diverse claims for attention, expertise, and time. The individual who prepared at a major research university and secures a position in a smaller, multipurpose university may well have considerable adjustment and learning to undergo. In such situations experienced faculty can serve as mentors, providing neophytes to the campus with ways of meeting the many demands and expectations without losing their valued zest for scholarship. Older faculty members would thus be participating in activities with clear impact on the future, a potentially powerful experience for those in the years during which they are considering and reflecting on their own contributions to the field and those with whom they have worked. Finally, such a practice explicates the view that education is a profession in which its members help one another and show concern for shared issues and problems. The wisdom and experience of older faculty could be honored, thus meeting a developmental need. One can envision situations in which young faculty, more skilled and knowledgeable in research, serve as the teachers of their elders, while the latter serve as mentors for the young as they assume their faculty roles.

Clearly, then, one of the vital concerns for teacher educators, graduate or undergraduate, is the matter of the growing volume of useful knowledge based on carefully designed and executed research studies. Teacher education faculty must become thoroughly familiar with the literature, its strengths and weaknesses; assist in promulgating research findings that seem important; involve preservice and in-service students in learning activities incorporating findings of merit; and provide an environment that fosters intellectual analysis of research and its findings. Curricula, at the very least, must be informed by this research and, at best, infused with it. Such intents raise several pointed questions for faculty development.

- How does one overcome what has been for some a historic disinclination to regard educational research as meaningful?
- How does one ensure that all faculty who instruct prospective and practicing professionals have the skills necessary to understand the extant and emerging research? A profession much given to show-and-tell, to anecdotal presentations, will require a reorientation. A shift in emphasis from an experience-based curriculum to a research-based curriculum is necessary. Faculty development efforts could aid this shift.

- How does one sponsor and promote faculty research that is respectable from a scholarly standpoint and, at the same time, vital to the institution's clients? The probability of potent research is greatly enhanced by faculty doing quality work in collaboration with their clients in the schools, an activity that should be sanctioned as part of faculty development efforts.

- How does one accomplish all of the above without producing a climate of research-based determinism? A view of research that is itself developmental must be presented. Within teacher education institutions, research must be regarded as the best knowledge currently available to support specific activities, but also subject to change and refinement.

The answers to these and related questions will vary from institution to institution. Those institutions having resident experts might well use their own talents to have an impact on other faculties in other institutions; all institutions must, however, provide for the development of faculty so that they become fully familiar with the best research in their fields.

Conclusion and Recommendations

This chapter has described some of the conditions that affect faculty development. The conditions have been in place a long time; they are simply more acute in the late 1980s. The demands for change, improvement, and growth are too insistent and politically forceful not to have impact. Consequently, wise leaders of higher education institutions will effectively utilize people, programs, external supports, and other resources to promote the well-being of their organizations through vital faculty development. In such manner will the last third of many faculty careers be enriched by productive and meaningful work and the first third of new faculty careers be powerfully begun. The following remarks are recommendations for presidents, vice presidents, and other institutional leaders to consider for the development of teacher education faculty; the recommendations are in the context of the work of these faculty, part of which is common to all higher education faculty and part of which is peculiar to teacher education faculty.

1. *Recognize achievement.* Despite what some university leaders may think about their efforts to recognize faculty achievement, the lament of faculty is "No one around here knows or values what I do. When I go someplace, people have heard of my work, but here no one seems to know about it." Campus "stars" get recognition; more average faculty members with occasional achievements rarely do. Effective public relations, timely and pointed announcements, special awards, and personal notes to faculty are only a few of the ways in which individual achievement can be recognized. Such efforts honor the individual and enhance the quality of life in the institution.

2. *Allocate funds for faculty development.* Most businesses and industries provide for the development of their valued employees through advanced education, travel, seminars, special training and learning institutes, employment exchanges, and new assignments. Higher education leaders may *think* they do such things by the sabbatical policies, but—as observed earlier—a sabbatical is often solely an academic development effort, important but not providing the flexibility and variety needed. An allocation of .2 percent for faculty development on an institutional budget of $300 million would produce $600,000; an allocation of .02 percent, $60,000. Such funds, available whether or not faculty had sabbatical leaves or other institutional support, would raise faculty morale, provide for imaginative proposals, demonstrate commitment to faculty, and foster significant growth and development. Augmented fiscal resources for teacher education faculty development would have a very positive effect on faculty inasmuch as teacher education has been historically underfunded in nearly all institutions.

3. *Provide programs that recognize developmental needs among faculty.* Elementary and secondary education, and to a more limited extent undergraduate education, have paid increasing attention to developmental literature as they have adapted instruction and programs. If faculty development is to be meaningful, institutional leaders must provide programs that

explicitly recognize differences among faculty in career stage, professional needs, and changing personal goals.

4. *Provide realistic and obtainable opportunities for faculty to exchange positions with faculty in other institutions.* Many institutions "allow" this practice, but they rarely promote and even more rarely provide the logistical support necessary. Since the majority of faculty members are in the second half of their careers and have fewer family responsibilities, the next few years are ideal times to promote exchanges. For example, a professor with a specialty in early childhood education who teaches in a rural area would be enriched both personally and professionally by the opportunity to teach in an urban area; similarly, his or her counterpart in an urban institution would benefit by going from urban to rural.

5. *Promote opportunities for faculty to assume different positions within the institution itself.* In such instances both the institution and the individual would profit. For example, a faculty member might spend a year in the office of the dean of students or might assist in managing the graduate college or a comparable organization. The institution stands to gain in a variety of ways; for instance, a faculty member in a new position might ask pertinent questions about policies and practices that may have been unquestioned for years.

6. *Promote opportunities for faculty to assume roles in the lower schools.* Learning about current schooling is both a passive and an active activity, passive as in reading and active as in spending time in schools. Many faculty might spend more time in schools—working with teachers, observing children, teaching classes—if the higher education system truly supported such activities. Faculty in most institutions quickly learn at promotion, tenure, and salary times that such activities are not well acknowledged. As a way of developing faculty strengths and collaboration between higher education and the lower schools, faculty should be encouraged to take positions in the lower schools for a period of time—with the understanding that they will be rewarded rather than penalized for their efforts.

7. *Legitimize the direct work with the schools by recognizing and valuing it.* Teacher education faculty spend large

amounts of time and energy working with schools in direct ways that aid the education of the young and promote the well-being of the schools. Generally, such activities are acknowledged as something that education units do on campus; they are rarely acknowledged with, for example, the kudos accorded to professors of engineering who may work with local industry to develop a new product. University leadership could promote the welfare of faculty and the public good by genuine, sustained articulation of the importance of the role filled by education faculty in their direct work with schools.

8. *Develop a mentor system whereby mature faculty work with new faculty.* Older faculty occasionally think that they are neither needed nor valued in the institution beyond the performance of duties and tasks they have long since mastered. The late 1980s and the 1990s promise to be a time of modest growth in the numbers of education faculty at many institutions. There will thus be a need to enculturate new members. This need can best be met by mature faculty working with young faculty in deliberative ways.

9. *Recognize program development as a viable and respected intellectual activity, worthy of academic respect and reward.* Nearly all higher education faculty devote time and energy to program development; given current demands for educational reform, teacher education faculty must give particular attention to program development during the next decade. An equitable system would recognize and value such activities, when they are performed with academic rigor, as a legitimate part of a faculty member's scholarly pursuits.

In the final analysis, institutional leaders need vision, wisdom, and perseverence: vision, to imagine what individuals, seemingly locked in place and time, might become and do; wisdom, to know what might be most potent for and attainable by the many; perseverence, to believe steadfastly in the richness, diversity, and potential of human beings. The possibility of dramatic improvement in the preparation of the nation's teachers and in the lives of their teachers is greatly enhanced by the understanding and application of the knowledge of adult development to institutional faculty development efforts.

7   *David C. Smith*

Redesigning the Curriculum
in Teacher Education

Thirty years ago a teacher with a bachelor's degree was considered an educated individual. Today a far greater proportion of the population has graduated from college, and many occupations that once required only a high school diploma now require a college degree. Consequently, teacher preparation programs, which have endured for over a half century as baccalaureate programs at some institutions, simply are not viewed as adequate preparation for teachers. In addition, better, more consistent, and more reliable research data relating teacher behaviors to pupil performance are now at the disposal of teacher educators. The findings of hundreds of studies have been synthesized and put into a form whereby they can be better utilized. Much of that information can be incorporated into teacher preparation programs. A curriculum based on that information is proposed in this chapter.

Components of the Curriculum

Table 1 gives an overview of the various components of the proposed curriculum for teacher preparation programs. The following sections contain more detailed, but not exhaustive, descriptions.

Table 1. Curriculum Design in Teacher Education.

Component	Area	
	Elementary	Secondary
General Education	Broad study in the liberal arts and sciences and in the fine arts.	
Preeducation	In-depth study in appropriate social science areas.	
Subject-Matter Background	Additional study in the teaching fields found in the elementary school curriculum.	Completion of an undergraduate degree in the teaching field. Very limited study in education.
Foundational Professional Studies	Study in fields of education that support professional practice in education across teaching fields and age levels. This area includes study in educational psychology, tests and measurement, and computer applications.	
Generic Professional Studies	Study in classroom practice and related matters that cut across subject matter and age levels. Such topics as the research that directly relates teaching behaviors to student performance and school district expectations are included.	
Subject-Specific Professional Studies	Methodology in teaching the various disciplines in the elementary school.	Methodology in teaching the disciplines in the secondary school.
Clinical Studies	The application of professional knowledge to practice at various levels of sophistication and in a variety of settings. Occurs throughout the professional program.	

General Education. The general education component includes at least two years of the humanities, sciences, mathematics, social sciences, and fine arts. A comprehensive general education background should be required of teachers for all age levels and for all subject fields. This requirement is based on the long-standing, and still valid, proposition that teachers should serve as exemplars of broadly, not narrowly, educated individuals.

Specifically, prospective teachers should study the history and development of Western civilization. They should also have a basic understanding of the history and culture of Asia and Africa. They should study English literature, composition, and linguistics and should demonstrate that they can communicate effectively, both in writing and orally. In this connection the institution should establish a meaningful writing examination as a condition for graduation from a teacher preparation program. In addition, substantive study in the sciences should be mandatory. The physical sciences, biological sciences, astronomy, and physical geography should be available to meet this requirement. Study in mathematics, including statistics, also should be required, as should study in computer science, including computer literacy and applications. Finally, substantial study in the social sciences—including political science, government, economics, sociology, psychology, and anthropology—should be required.

Since teacher candidates should bring an academic background to higher education that permits them to study effectively at a postsecondary level, remedial work should not be counted toward the completion of general education requirements.

Preeducation. A preeducation requirement that builds on and goes beyond the general education requirement in the social sciences should be placed on those individuals who wish to become teachers. It should reflect study in areas of the social sciences that are particularly appropriate for educators and that offer deeper insight into contemporary social conditions relevant to the schools. It should include study in such areas as sociology of the family, cultural anthropology, social psychology, computer literacy, and urban sociology.

Subject-Matter Background. Individuals enrolled in contemporary teacher preparation programs must master the subject matter that they intend to teach, and their mastery must far exceed that of the most advanced of their secondary students.

Individuals aspiring to become secondary teachers should complete an undergraduate degree in their teaching field. The equivalent is not sufficient. Individuals preparing for careers in teaching at the secondary school level should be qualified to teach in more than one field. Some will contend that such an expectation is unrealistic and, hence, undesirable; however, it does reflect the nature of teaching assignments in the secondary school and, as a result, is highly desirable, if not essential. Possible exceptions may prevail in English and mathematics, where teachers may be assigned full teaching loads. The establishment of such requirements may make it possible to reduce the number of teachers, otherwise qualified, who are currently teaching one or more classes outside the field(s) in which they are licensed.

Course work in the teaching field should focus on those aspects of the subject that are taught in secondary schools. For example, students majoring in English who intend to become teachers would take most of their courses in composition and linguistics and fewer in the various forms of literature, which may have little or no direct application to the secondary school. In similar fashion, individuals majoring in mathematics who expect to become secondary teachers should perhaps be able to demonstrate an unusual command of aspects of the subject, such as algebra and trigonometry, that are taught in secondary schools. In this connection teacher educators who are specialists in teaching specific areas of the curriculum could help faculty in the various arts and science departments design a program more conducive to the preparation of effective secondary school teachers.

Students preparing to become teachers need to demonstrate strong scholarship. An overall grade point average approaching 3.0 should be required as a condition for admission to teacher education. Furthermore, that grade point average should be maintained as a condition for remaining in the program and for graduation.

Individuals preparing to become elementary teachers should also be expected to possess greater depth in their subject-matter background than is currently required. These individuals should major in education, with increased requirements in fields of study reflected in the elementary school curriculum. These increased requirements should be substantial and broad based. A major in liberal arts reflects a depth of study in one area or related areas but rarely permits the breadth of study that should be required of an elementary teacher.

Certification as an elementary teacher should not be possible with the acquisition of the undergraduate degree, since expansion of the study in the various teaching fields will render it impossible to complete an acceptable professional preparation program. Concentrations of study in at least two areas of the curriculum found in the elementary school should be required beyond those specified in the general education requirements. At least one such concentration should be in an area outside the school, college, or department of education; however, individuals preparing to become elementary teachers should be permitted to complete one concentration of study in reading, special education, or media and technology. In addition, prospective elementary school teachers should be required to take at least two laboratory science courses, to help them become more knowledgeable and comfortable in dealing with the tools of science in the classroom: one course in the biological sciences and one in the physical sciences. An introductory course in statistics, offered in the statistics or mathematics department as a prerequisite to study in tests and measurement in professional education, also should be required.

Professional Education. Four distinct elements are included in the professional component in teacher preparation programs.

Foundational studies include those studies in education that undergird the preparation of all teachers, regardless of the subject matter to be taught or the age of the pupil: computer applications in education (with some adaptation made to grade level and field); computer skills and applications useful to teachers (such as record keeping and word processing); educational psychology and adolescent psychology or child growth and development; and tests and measurement, including the interpretation and reporting of standardized tests and teacher-constructed tests. In addition, such topics as the legal rights and responsibilities of teachers and pupils and basic education law (often not included in teacher preparation programs) are included among foundational studies. Although a full course in school law may not be necessary in a preservice teacher preparation program, beginning teachers need to know a sufficient amount to avoid becoming legally vulnerable in the classroom.

The generic element of professional education deals with the study of those aspects of teaching that are neither age specific nor content specific. Prospective teachers must become familiar with all the relevant research—or, at least, the best available conventional wisdom—on practices associated with effective teaching. Protocol films may be useful in providing students with opportunities to demonstrate that they can identify specific research-based teacher behaviors in the classroom. The generic element also includes research-based material on instructional planning, classroom management, the delivery of instruction, observation, communication, evaluation, counseling with pupils and parents, and the teaching of higher-order thinking skills in the classroom (an important area either overlooked or underemphasized in many teacher preparation programs).

The subject-specific element of professional education includes the study of such content as the teaching of reading or mathematics in the primary or the secondary school. In secondary teacher preparation, the content should be specific to the methodology and materials (both print and nonprint materials) appropriate to teaching the various subjects in the secondary school—including, but not necessarily limited to, science, mathematics, the social sciences, English, and physical education. It should include a laboratory component, so that students can acquire direct experience in teaching the subject; microteaching experience has been found particularly valuable in this instance. Students also should acquire limited experience in a school setting.

The subject-specific element in the preparation program for elementary teachers is more comprehensive and time-consuming than that required of secondary teachers, since elementary teachers have broader teaching responsibilities. Unfortunately, there is little transferability from one area of the curriculum to another; that is, the methods and materials necessary to teach reading effectively have little relationship to the methods or materials available for effectively teaching science in the elementary school.

Consistent with the practice advocated for secondary teachers, each of the methods courses for elementary teachers should contain a laboratory component. The laboratory component should include microteaching experience, so that the students themselves may observe their teaching techniques and mannerisms. It should also include, under close supervision and with generous feedback, limited direct experience in teaching small groups of school-age children.

The clinical element of professional education relates to those aspects of the program where students apply the knowledge and skills they have learned to an actual classroom situation. The activities included may range from observation in a structured situation (for example, a situation shown on film) to teaching a full class of students. There should be a clear progression in the level of expectation and the complexity of the teaching required. For example, in learning how to teach a concept, students might progress from observation, to microteaching, to teaching an individual, to teaching a small group, to teaching an entire class. They might focus on the content to be taught or on various aspects of teaching, such as observation, planning, classroom management, the presentation of content, or evaluation. A structured experience, which might be presented through videotape or other means or acquired in a "real" school setting, should be included.

Carefully developed materials, such as films, permit students to identify teacher behaviors associated with effective teaching. First, students should learn those behaviors; second, they should be able to observe and identify positive and negative teacher behaviors in the classroom; third, they should be able to practice in a microteaching setting, so that they can observe their own behavior; fourth, they should be able to practice effective teaching techniques in an actual classroom with abundant feedback. An early field experience is desirable because it can help students either confirm their commitment to pursue a career in education or make a more appropriate career selection. It is also useful in helping students establish more realistic expectations for themselves and for their students.

The clinical pedagogical element for individuals preparing to become secondary teachers should provide experience in all fields in which they are to be certified to teach. Preferably, those experiences should be acquired at more than one teaching level and in more than one school. The clinical pedagogical element for prospective elementary teachers should provide experience in teaching the subject matter in each major area of the elementary school curriculum at more than one grade level and in more than one school. Preferably, the experiences should occur at different socioeconomic levels.

The President's Role in Curriculum Development

Although presidents and chief academic officers usually do not have the background and knowledge necessary to speak with authority about the curriculum in teacher education, they do have enormous power to influence decisions on the campus and to influence policy makers at a state level or, occasionally, even at the national level. It follows, then, that presidents have more than a role in the improvement of the curriculum in teacher education; they carry a responsibility as well.

Presidents should give positive visibility to schools, colleges, and departments of education (SCDEs) by attaching value to the preparation of teachers; bringing attention to program improvement activities in the SCDE; commenting on research activities in the SCDE; and recognizing the activities of faculty who are involved in the leadership of various professional educational organizations, as well as faculty who are providing inservice training programs to practitioners in the area or state. It is reasonable for presidents to request information that will help them provide visibility to the SCDE and improve its status on the campus. If the SCDE cannot provide the president with the needed information, it may be concluded that the SCDE has, or is, a problem on the campus.

The president can also make clear to the SCDE that he or she is an uncompromising and unyielding advocate for stronger and better teacher preparation programs—programs that address the concerns expressed by the various reformers who seek improvement in teacher education. Often educators in the SCDE tend to underestimate the level of outside dissatisfaction over teacher education and to defend current programs. Presidents can exert leadership to help college faculty and administrators understand that the issue is not the quality of what has occurred in the past but the necessity to design new teacher preparation programs that will equip the teachers of the twenty-first century to educate youth so that they can function effectively in the Information Age.

Presidents should avoid the temptation—perhaps stronger in smaller institutions—to become involved in the details of curriculum development. Although the president can support the development of a stronger curriculum in teacher education, the role of "super-dean" is likely to be counterproductive. Probably the most constructive position a president can take is to be involved in the curriculum process in education at the same level of specificity as for any other professional program on the campus.

The president should demand that the SCDE document, quantitatively, the quality of its programs. One indication of program strength is national accreditation. It is appropriate for the president to expect the SCDE to seek and acquire national accreditation in education. Indeed, an institution committed to strong academic programs and interested in being recognized for its quality should strive for national accreditation in all disciplines and areas where programs may be accredited by an agency recognized by the Council on Postsecondary Accreditation (COPA). In the final analysis, the best judgments regarding program strength can be made through nationally accepted standards and by a panel of peers in the discipline.

When institutional self-interest conflicts with the self-interest of the SCDE, institutional self-interest will, and should, prevail. In such circumstances a strong, capable president most concerned with the long-term interest of the institution will act decisively and be prepared to close weak programs.

Finally, presidents and chief academic officers should recognize some of the problems inherent in SCDEs. For example, the design of teacher preparation programs is such that they cannot generate large lower-division undergraduate classes, which capture large numbers of student credit hours and thus help to ensure the quality of upper-division offerings, as is the case in such liberal arts and science disciplines as psychology and sociology. Another problem is that the clinical aspects of teacher education are inherently expensive and labor intensive, and these expensive programs must be paid for out of the general budget—which also supports the total institution. In probably no other field is virtually the entire professional constituency composed of individuals deriving their resources from the state. Consequently, there is an ultimate conflict of interest in that, when professional associations that are made up of K–12 educators support colleges of education, they run the risk of reducing appropriations to the institutions by whom they are employed.

Conclusion

The curriculum in teacher education, as we know it in the United States, is not flawed in design but is clearly inadequate in scope. If education is to assume the status of a profession, greater and more sophisticated content must be incorporated into preservice teacher preparation programs. The curriculum specified in this chapter can be expected to challenge intellectually capable and committed individuals. It can also be expected to be time-consuming. The typical teacher preparation curriculum cannot accommodate a rigorous general education component, expanded requirements for study in the teaching field, and a more rigorous, research-based, and clinically oriented pedagogical component and still be accomplished in four academic years. Nevertheless, if teachers are to perform as professionals, the expectations described are not unreasonable.

A review of the evolution of several professions demonstrates that increases in salary and social esteem are preceded by increases in the duration and level of professional preparation. Minimal and marginal increases in the scope of professional preservice preparation for teachers are simply unacceptable. Additions to the typical preservice teacher preparation programs currently in existence are simply inadequate and inappropriate. What is needed is a major revision of the content and the manner in which it is taught. In reality, the curriculum needed to prepare fully qualified teachers requires an academic program of at least five years' duration.

8

Robert L. Egbert

Identifying Resources
Needed to Improve
Teacher Education

Until relatively recently many teacher educators, John Dewey
notwithstanding, seemed to assume that college and university
students could listen to lectures and thereby learn how children
learn and how teachers teach. As a result, most colleges and universities have treated teacher education as a low-cost program,
one in which the professional preparation courses could be
taught as lecture courses or lecture and total-class discussion
courses, much as those in social sciences and humanities frequently are taught. As we have learned more about teaching and
learning processes, the tradition of conducting professional education courses almost entirely through lectures has largely dis-
appeared in good teacher education programs, much as the lecture method in architecture and engineering has been replaced
by lectures combined with laboratory and studio experiences.

Because we know that teachers must be prepared by a
combination of theory and practice running through the entire
program (Goodlad, 1986), teacher educators are changing their
preparation programs to accommodate what we have learned.
However, preparing teachers in such programs requires both
additional equipment and materials and more faculty as well as
faculty with different backgrounds of education and experi-

ence. Unfortunately, the funding patterns necessary to provide essential equipment and materials, as well as faculty who are qualified for clinical programs of teacher education, have not kept pace with what we know is needed. The purpose of this chapter is to describe patterns of resources that we now realize are required to prepare teachers.

In Chapter Seven of this volume, David Smith outlines characteristics of good teacher education programs; the present chapter builds from that description in discussing the human and material resources required for such programs and tying them to the world of practice. Although this chapter begins with a brief description of the current inadequate resources for teacher education, it gives primary emphasis to explaining what is needed to meet changing program requirements. In addition to describing the resources required for the actual conduct of programs, the chapter acknowledges two related resource matters: program development and the recruitment and support of qualified candidates, especially minorities. The final portion of the chapter emphasizes that the express support of the president is the single most important resource a teacher education program can have. Without strong leadership, both within the program and at the presidential level, no amount of material help directly to the program will meet its needs.

Present Status of Funding for Teacher Education

As noted, programs to prepare teachers typically are funded on the same basis as liberal arts lecture courses. A number of authors have written about this problem. Peseau, for instance (1979, 1980, 1982, 1984), has documented both the actual and relative funding made available to teacher education programs in state universities and land-grant colleges. Peseau uses two concepts—adequacy and equity—to describe program funding. Adequacy asks whether the funds provided for a program are sufficient to meet the program's needs; equity asks whether a college or university has divided the funds available to it in a manner that is fair to its various programs.

Peseau concludes that in the state universities and land-grant colleges he studied, teacher education has been the victim of inadequate funding. He found, for example, that only in nine of the fifty-one universities in his sample was the direct cost of instruction as much as the cost for educating public school students. This finding parallels that of Bowen (1980), who reported that in 1976–77 a number of colleges and universities were providing instruction at a cost per student of from $1,000 to $1,700, well below the $1,782 national average expenditure then being provided for the education of elementary and secondary students. Furthermore, in thirty of the fifty-one public universities studied by Peseau (1982), the teacher education students paid more than half of the direct costs of instruction. Teacher education students paid even more than the total direct instructional costs in eight of these universities.

Although part of the problem in providing the funds needed for teacher education is with the overall shortage of financial resources available to colleges and universities, another part is related to the division made of the funds that they receive—Peseau's issue of equity. For example, Peseau (1984) learned from a detailed study of the funding pattern of one major state university that the cost per weighted student credit hour for education was $45.98; for engineering, $96.13; and for business, $57.20. In this instance, even if the state provided the university with adequate funds for instruction, teacher education would be placed at a major financial disadvantage when compared with engineering and business administration.

Although the Peseau figures are important, they deal only with state universities and land-grant colleges, perhaps the set of higher education institutions best able to fund teacher education. Thus, Peseau's data do not reveal the actual extent of teacher education's underfunding. Easily documentable cases indicate the nature of the resource crisis in certain other teacher education programs: (1) The head of a teacher education program in a liberal arts college cannot purchase a $10 item because it was not put in the budget. (2) A senior professor teaches three three-credit courses *and* supervises sixteen student teachers by driving to locations from twenty-five to three hundred miles from campus. (3) Professors must purchase their own chalk and pay for copying syllabi and other materials for class. (4) One overhead projector serves the entire department, and professors must schedule its use and carry it to class with them. (5) The department has no access to video equipment for use in either on-campus microteaching or other clinical work or in supervising student teachers.

Such examples are merely the worst. Almost no teacher educators have access to equipment and materials essential to the high-quality clinical work described by Smith. Certainly, few teacher education programs have instructional equipment and facilities and a faculty/student ratio equivalent to that for their football and basketball teams.

Estimates of Resources Needed for Teacher Education

Several general statements have been made about the support needed for teacher education. Peseau (1982) has suggested, for instance, specific student/faculty ratios (22:1 for lower division, 15:1 for upper division, and 12:1 for master's level), levels of operating budgets (for example, $4.50 per master's-level student credit hour), and support staff/faculty ratios (1:5 at the undergraduate level and 1:4 at the master's level).

After a detailed study of three teacher education programs (a large college of education, a medium-sized college of education, and an undergraduate department of education in a small, denominational, liberal arts college), Nutter (1986) tentatively concludes that the two greatest financial needs in teacher education programs, in terms of absolute cost, are for additional personnel and regular operating funds. She estimates that, at a minimum, the typical teacher education program needs about a 30 percent increase in personnel support. She also estimates that, to achieve excellence, teacher education programs typically need at least a 60 percent increase in general operating expenses.

The Peseau reports give general guidance against which colleges and universities can examine the resources that they make available to teacher education. The Nutter report suggests dimensions that higher education administrators should consider as they study where their teacher education programs may need additional resources. To add detail to the Peseau and Nutter reports, this chapter builds from Smith's program description and, to a lesser extent, the national standards used by the National Council for Accreditation of Teacher Education (1982) in identifying somewhat more specific human and material resource needs within teacher education programs. Although I have listed quite specific items, I have sometimes avoided recommending either quantities or ratios because of the context variables that influence the need for numbers and ratios.

Reasons for Special Funding Needs

At least three factors cause teacher education programs to require special funding beyond that provided for traditional lecture courses: (1) Each step of the program must have laboratory and/or field experiences, and each teacher candidate must have direct faculty supervision and guidance in these experiences. (2) Specialized equipment is needed: video machines for analysis and critique of the teacher candidate's performance in campus clinical settings and in schools; microcomputers for showing students how to use technology in both simple and complex learning tasks; and laboratories for producing and using slides, transparencies, and other teaching aids. (3) The faculty required in high-quality teacher education programs—faculty who have skills and experience in teaching, research, and supervision—are in high demand in other positions. Incentives are needed to attract and keep such faculty in teacher education.

Even though some professional courses in teacher education—an educational foundations course, for instance—are based primarily in the college classroom, each course should be an amalgam of theory and the real world to which the theory pertains. Otherwise, theory, practice, and the real-world context of teaching will never come together (Goodlad, 1986). Even the traditional educational foundations courses should provide related field experiences that will enable each student to draw the world of symbols and the world from which those symbols are derived more closely together. Most teacher education programs

now have clinical and field experiences associated with all or almost all the courses that precede student teaching. Such courses
more closely resemble the studio courses required for architecture and art students and the clinical practice courses in social
work and speech pathology than they do traditional lecture
courses.

Smith's chapter describes teacher preparation programs in
which prospective elementary and secondary teachers acquire
knowledge of abstract concepts and learn to use these concepts
and related observational and teaching skills in both laboratory
and classroom settings. The processes that he has outlined suggest a progression in the development of knowledge and skills.
Steps in this progression are essentially as follows:

1. Observing and Analyzing
    a. Viewing films, tapes, and slides to learn to identify
        and analyze student and teacher behavior
    b. Observing in classrooms and analyzing those obser-
        vations
2. Teaching Lessons and Units
    a. Planning lessons and teaching them in laboratory
        and microteaching sessions
    b. Planning and teaching lessons and units in class-
        rooms
3. Teaching Under Supervision
    a. Student teaching under supervision on a continuing
        basis
    b. Internship

The four processes listed in steps 1 and 2 should precede
student teaching; they should be an integral part of the laboratory or clinical portion of the human development, educational
psychology, and methods courses. However, these four processes should not be considered completely discrete and sequential. Instead, they should be interactive, with increased experience and competence on one dimension preparing the student
for further experience on another. Observing, analyzing, and receiving feedback can be practiced much more efficiently in a

laboratory than in a classroom; however, the laboratory practice cannot replace the need for observing and analyzing in classrooms. The two complement each other. Viewing and analyzing films, tapes, and slides, then, should occur in a laboratory setting; on the other hand, observing students in a classroom and analyzing these observations requires being in a school. Again, these processes should be interactive, not sequential. As students increase their ability to deal with more complex levels through actual classroom experience as well as further didactic instruction, they need added opportunities to learn through viewing films, tapes, and slides.

Students' learning of teaching behaviors is analogous to their learning of observing behaviors. Thus, certain teaching behaviors also are best learned in carefully controlled and monitored circumstances apart from a classroom full of students. In some instances such structured rehearsals should occur before the prospective teacher tests his or her skills in the field. In other instances actual classroom experience may be important to help the student understand the laboratory task. Extensive experiences in planning and teaching lessons and units in microteaching as well as in a classroom should occur before the traditional student teaching or internship experience.

Both student teaching and internships occur in the field. However, even as they take place, there is need for reference back to films, tapes, slides, and other materials to help illustrate particular points in understanding what is taking place in the classroom.

Each of the six processes listed requires extensive, specialized supervision and the availability and use of equipment. These human and material needs are described below.

Human Resource Requirements

Courses in teacher education that include laboratory or clinical experiences either should have restricted enrollments (no more than fifteen to eighteen students per section), to permit the professor to give individual attention to each student's laboratory and field experiences, or there should be separate lecture and laboratory sections in which the laboratory section enrollments do not exceed fifteen to eighteen. The student/ supervisor ratio should not exceed fifteen students for each full-time faculty supervisor. That is, supervising five student teachers should count at least as the equivalent of one three-credit-hour class, and the supervisor should spend as much time and energy in the supervision of the five students as he or she would normally spend in preparing and teaching a three-credit-hour class. If extensive travel time is required, fewer student teachers should be assigned to the supervisor.

Regardless of the student/teacher ratio and restrictions on program coverage, a critical mass of teacher education faculty is necessary. Several professors are needed to provide competent teaching of the range of content described in Chapters Two and Seven and to give students experience with multiple perspectives about teaching and learning. A critical mass of professors also is necessary to enable faculty and students to engage in productive inquiry and to provide opportunities for stimulating dialogue among faculty members and between faculty and students (Goodlad, 1986). A single level or type of program—for example, elementary, secondary, or special education—should not be attempted without at least four faculty members whose primary commitment is teacher education. If two or more levels or types of programs are offered, at least five full-time faculty members—faculty who are especially competent, not those who are inexperienced or minimally trained—should be available exclusively to teacher education.

Some major universities have employed as teacher education faculty only persons whose primary interest is not the preparation of teachers. Furthermore, they often have developed priorities and reward systems that make it difficult to assign regular professors to teach in their teacher preparation programs. Such universities employ graduate assistants, instructors, part-time faculty, and junior, untenured faculty to conduct the major portions of their teacher education programs. This practice is not appropriate (Goodlad, 1986).

No college or university, even those that are committed to professional education, should feel obligated to prepare teachers. Functions other than the preparation of teachers may be more appropriate to the mission of certain universities. Such universities should limit their scope of activities to those appropriate to their mission rather than maintain teacher education programs that are essentially conducted entirely by graduate students whose primary interest is earning the money necessary to prepare themselves for reseach careers.

Much has been written about traits that are important for teacher educators (see, for instance, National Commission for Excellence in Teacher Education, 1985; Lanier and others, 1986; Lanier and Little, 1985; Carnegie Task Force on Teaching as a Profession, 1986; National Council for Accreditation of Teacher Education, 1982). High value is placed on successful experience as a teacher in K-12 schools. Also valued are intelligence, knowledge of both subject taught and pedagogical principles, ability to apply pedagogical principles, and competence in the conduct and utilization of educational research. Professional educators with these characteristics are in demand in K-12 school systems as well as in colleges and universities. Furthermore, the salaries available to them frequently are substantially higher in K-12 schools than in higher education. Thus, colleges and universities must be prepared to compete not only with each other for first-rate teacher education faculty but also with the schools for these same people.

In Chapter Six of this volume, Edward Ducharme has outlined the need for faculty development programs for teacher educators and has described important elements in such programs. Continuing development of faculty demands resources. Colleges and universities that prepare teachers should certainly plan a faculty development program as an integral part of its budget.

Equipment Needs

Video playback equipment and film and slide projectors are needed for both demonstration and student practice purposes in a clinical teacher education program; and students need to have quiet space set aside where they can view and code videotapes, films, and slides. Videocameras and playback equipment also must be available for microteaching and other preliminary teaching experiences. In short, a pedagogical laboratory is as important to education professors and students as engineering laboratories are to engineering professors and their students.

For the field experiences described earlier, either the supervisor must have access to a portable videocamera or there must be video equipment in the schools where the lessons or units are taught and where student teaching takes place and internships are served. Videotapes of teaching sessions must be made, so that the supervising professor, the student (intern), and, when possible, the cooperating teacher can view and analyze them. In addition, recently developed monitoring devices—including portable computers and keyboards that permit direct entry of coded behaviors—soon will be important equipment adjuncts for both the student and the instructor in laboratory and field settings. No professor or student should find it difficult or inconvenient to use video and audio equipment, because these are the tools that make clinical teacher preparation programs possible.

Other instructional equipment needed in all good teacher preparation programs includes equipment for the preparation and use of transparencies and, of course, computers. Computers are far more readily available in schools than in teacher education programs, and middle-class children have greater access to computers than either schools or teacher education programs do. Most schools have computer specialists on their faculties, and classroom teachers must be able to instruct students in the operation and use of computers. Thus, each teacher education student should be able to use a computer's word-processing capability and its other functions at a level necessary for instructing students at the level he or she teaches.

Like equipment in other fields, equipment used by teacher educators wears out or becomes obsolete. Equipment that was the best available just a few years ago now is outdated, especially in the developing fields of video and computer technology. Provision should be made to replace worn and outdated equipment for teacher education, just as it is for other fields.

Other Special Needs of Teacher Education

When needs of the moment are especially great, focusing attention on the future becomes particularly difficult. However, if we are to achieve the reforms necessary in teacher education, resources must be set aside for two functions that do not receive the support they need. These functions are (1) program development in teacher education and (2) state and national support to ameliorate the projected shortage of minority teachers.

Program Development. Although teacher educators draw upon a common body of knowledge, each faculty must develop its program to meet both the philosophy of the group and the needs of its students and the schools where they will teach. Because of the unique features of each teacher education program, major reformulation of a program requires intensive effort and a great deal of time for designing, working through the details, and testing of both individual portions and the overall program. In this period when schools are depending on colleges and universities to improve the way they educate teachers, program tinkering will not suffice. To do more than tinker requires resources. Colleges and universities that are serious about improving their programs will provide the essential campus-level leadership and make financial and other resources available for program reformulation—for providing faculty release time, employing personnel, purchasing equipment and supplies, employing outside consultant help, traveling to visit other programs, and doing the other tasks necessary to successful program development. An interesting example of major program reform is provided by Grambling State University (Mills, forthcoming).

Recruiting and Educating Minority Teachers. In Chapter Four of this volume, David and Douglas Imig describe the general and minority population trends in this country. Their figures suggest that, if we sort teacher supply and demand into majority and minority teachers, most parts of the country will experience relatively little, if any, shortage of teachers among the majority population. Instead, there will be a dramatic shortage among minority teachers. This shortage poses an especially perplexing dilemma at a time when we have not come close to conquering the majority/minority issue of educational equity. Only if we have an enormous increase in the number of black, Hispanic, and other minority teachers can we hope to reduce the educational excellence gap that exists among the various subgroups of our population.

Summary and Discussion

Almost every major educational report of the last few years (for example, National Commission on Excellence in Education, 1983; Boyer, 1983; Goodlad, 1984) has emphasized the need for reforming teacher education. In addition, the report of the National Commission for Excellence in Teacher Education (1985) contains sixteen explicit recommendations for improving teacher education. Recommendations by the Holmes Group (Lanier and others, 1986) and the Carnegie Task Force on Teaching as a Profession (1986) essentially repeat some of the recommendations made in the commission's report and, in addition, advocate national testing, restructuring of the schools, and restriction of teacher education to the graduate level. Despite the many calls for reforming teacher education, only relatively minor changes appear to be under way in most programs. Only if there is consistent support from the college or university president is it likely that the teacher education faculty and its designated leaders will design and put in place the programs needed for the last part of this century. Presidential support is required to help the teacher education faculty, the public, and faculty members in other departments realize the continuing need for excellent teachers and the importance that the college (university) attaches to teacher education.

Teacher education is changing from a relatively low-cost lecture program (or lectures plus full-class discussions) to one requiring careful laboratory and clinical planning and supervision. This change necessitates increases in personnel and material budgets. Education professors must combine the traditional scholar and teacher competence with skills of clinical supervision. Such persons are needed in the practical world of K–12 schools; thus, colleges and universities must compete for a relatively small number of professionals who have the skills and competence required in two different professional worlds. In this respect, teacher education is like other professional fields, such as engineering, architecture, speech pathology, and clinical psychology. Furthermore, education professors need specialized equipment to assist them in their work.

Even in those colleges and universities with the greatest resources, the state universities and land-grant colleges, teacher education is underfunded. The underfunding in these institutions exists, whether judged by standards of adequacy (Do the resources meet the needs?) or equity (Does teacher education receive its fair share of the available resources?).

The education of teachers is too important to be treated casually. Thus, only if both the president and the board value teacher education enough to secure and allocate the necessary resources and provide the leadership essential to program success should they permit their college or university to educate teachers.

9

W. Ann Reynolds

What College and University Presidents Can Do to Strengthen Teacher Preparation

According to a large survey by Eisenberg and Grunwald (1985), successful Americans under the age of forty who chose careers in the sciences, arts and letters, or social service said that the most influential person in their lives was a teacher. (Mothers were most influential for those who chose entertainment fields; fathers, for those who chose business or politics.) The first civilian chosen to fly into space, now a true American martyr, was a teacher. The years of formal education remain pivotal in our lives. We identify ourselves quickly in groups by the schools we attended, and our anecdotes of those years reveal the impact of teachers on us. We Americans shed spouses readily, but never our Alma Mater. And teachers are the very essence of all our institutions of learning, from preschool through graduate school. Why, then, did our pride in teaching as a profession falter in the last twenty years?

The consequences have been drastic, humbling, and well known; they need not be recounted in detail here. They do include salaries far too low for teachers, unconstrained unionism, decreased control over curriculum and classroom activities, and diminished status in the community. Parents and community leaders tend to talk in general terms about the precipitous decline in the quality of teachers, and dozens of studies by learned groups have chronicled in various ways the decrement in our young people's fund of knowledge. Contrastingly, though, parents who currently have children in school are in general positive about the teachers they know personally.

It proved easy for those in higher education to submerge a traditional pride in teacher education. Institutions with the word *teachers* or *normal* in their title (including my own Kansas State Teachers College of Emporia) got rid of that appellation during the 1960s and 1970s. Christa McAuliffe, our mourned teacher-astronaut, received a B.S. from Framingham State College and an M.S. in education from Bowie State College, both former "teachers" colleges. The reasons given for the name changes were similar: rapid institutional growth to accommodate the post–World War II baby boom mandated a broadening in the mission of small state teachers colleges. Most of them became state universities in the process and worked quickly to erase any sense that their primary mission was to educate teachers.

It was not always so; we once took pride in the education of good teachers. During my undergraduate years in the biology department at Kansas State Teachers College, the department chairman, T. F. Andrews, kept a large map of Kansas above his desk. Colored pins went into every town for which the department prepared and dispatched a high school biology teacher. At the same time, it should be noted, the department performed the undergraduate preparation for many future physicians, dentists, medical technologists, and doctorates in the life sciences.

In later years the attention of university presidents was increasingly diverted by student activism, which led to more emphasis on the world beyond campus boundaries. The development of public-private partnerships, and more emphasis on private-sector as well as federal and state grant support, demanded increased presidential time and attention. Faculty research that drew funds to the university became more typically the benchmark of university success than did the preparation of outstanding students in any field. Yet, in spite of our nationwide orphaning of teacher education, programs persisted on our campuses. *No other* single professional curriculum remains as widespread or is offered by as many institutions nationwide. Almost thirteen hundred institutions offer teacher education programs; the constituency is a large and persistent one.

With the current shortage of teachers and the nationwide concern about the quality of teachers in our classrooms, educational quality has become a focus in issues of public policy. It would be hard today to find a state legislature that is not deliberating on bill after bill affecting the teacher. We, the faculty and administrators of our nation's colleges and universities, become outraged when our responsibility for and control of curriculum and graduation requirements come under legislative scrutiny and constraints. Indeed, it is doubtful that significant legislative intervention in the undergraduate experience and professional training would be tolerated in the fields of engineering, architecture, law, medicine, and even nursing. Does not our tolerance for external intervention in teacher preparation further document the university community's lack of proper concern for teaching? I believe that it does.

Now we must address a crisis in teacher preparation. In a climate of intense criticism of the teaching profession, and of increasing conservatism and materialism, we must try to recruit promising young people into teaching. Nationally, over 33 percent of bachelor's degrees are now awarded in business, engineering, or computer science. Our culture nurtures and grooms the "yuppie." Entry-level salaries and perquisites are motivating factors for our freshmen; the mass media are focused on young people who work to support a lifestyle, not those whose work *is* a lifestyle.

What is a weary college or university president to do? Happily, a lot, if he or she is willing.

It is a real revelation to sit down and talk about teachers and teaching with those who truly care. The constituency for teacher education is enormous and varied, uniformly eager to help, and yearning for attention to the teacher. County and city superintendents and principals, K–12 teachers, education administrators, and faculty—they are all rich with ideas. To tap these ideas, the university president should travel to the super-intendent's office, to the elementary and junior high, and to the education department. The president will then get a clear sense of the dimensions of the task and some potential solutions; of the attributes of good appointees to serve on advisory groups or task forces; and of an appropriate charge to the task force in order to gain maximum benefit, with minimum effort, from their deliberations.

Many benefits have come from my meetings with teacher educators around the state of California. For example, it emerged that an elementary education program offered by the California State University at Bakersfield was so popular that it was turning away candidates despite its high standards. It has become a model program for us, and one clearly deserving of more resources. Meetings with Harry Handler, superintendent of the Los Angeles Unified School District, led to several part-nership programs between the district and the California State University. For example, CSU and the Los Angeles Unified School District collaborated in the development of the Step to College Program, which enables promising minority high school juniors and seniors to take courses at a nearby CSU campus, thus encouraging their consideration of a university education and easing the transition from high school to college.

Specific widespread problems, such as inadequate recog-nition and support for faculty supervising student teachers, were identified through these discussions. As a result, a budget proposal to the state was developed to support improvement in student teaching, and funding was secured. In this way it was possible to demonstrate that commitment to educational im-provement was more than an abstraction.

To my surprise, there has been a significant halo effect accompanying the meetings and attention to teacher educa-tion. Because of the evidence of concern and support by the university's leadership, education faculty, department heads, and deans became more forthright and assertive on their own campuses about their aspirations and needs.

The culmination of this effort, of course, is the appoint-ment of a task force to review the status of teacher education and to generate recommendations for the optimal preparation of the teacher in a given university or college setting. Public school teachers and administrators, as well as faculty and administrators from other colleges in the university, must be represented along with education faculty in this review activity. Broad participation will go a long way toward ensuring acceptance and implementation of task force recommendations.

Mainstream Recommendations

The experience nationwide in revitalizing teacher education has yielded several common actions whose implementation has been helpful and made a real difference in teacher education:

1. Establishing rigorous entrance standards that require students to be in the top half of their undergraduate class for admission to teacher education programs.
2. Focusing on the multicultural education of prospective teachers, so that they can understand and effectively teach today's students.
3. Identifying the optimum core curriculum for education majors and ensuring that its content is challenging and relevant.
4. Ensuring that the subject-matter preparation of elementary teachers provides both depth and breadth, and is based on a strong liberal arts curriculum, and that secondary teachers are expert in the methodology and content of their disciplines.
5. Placing responsibility for the subject-matter competence of prospective teachers squarely on the shoulders of the academic department faculty.
6. Collaborating with exemplary teachers and administrators in the development of improved teacher education programs.

Partnerships with Public Schools

One of the freshest and most significant new achievements of the so-called "reform"—more accurately called "revival"—of teacher education has been the development of real partnerships between the college or university and nearby public schools. In our experience in California, such programs have benefited teacher preparation and also have provided real assistance to other sectors of the university. For example, teacher exchange programs provide enhanced visibility for the university and encourage outstanding students as well as in-service teachers to attend the university. In New York the City University of New York is overseeing the management of special secondary schools in minority neighborhoods. The university's faculty and resources provide a rich "in-kind" programmatic lift for the high school; the university and society benefit by lifting the aspirations of young people to increase their high school attainment, thus stemming the inordinately high dropout rate and improving the readiness of minority students to be successful college students.

Black students are attending college in diminishing numbers; the proportion of Hispanic students who attend college is not keeping pace with their increasing representation of college-age young people in the United States population. High school dropout rates are increasing, especially in predominantly minority schools in urban areas. The gains of the 1960s and 1970s with respect to minority access to higher education are eroding. It is in our own self-interest, and the fulfillment of a strong moral obligation, to unite with the public schools in attacking this problem. An increased determination to stress teacher education, and to recruit fine students into teaching, can work hand in glove with joint efforts between universities and public schools. Examples of these joint efforts in California between the California State University and public schools include the following:

- A collaborative effort to identify the optimum core curriculum for teacher education programs.
- Training programs on clinical supervision for K–12 and university faculty who supervise student teachers.
- Community-based centers through which laboratory activities for university students and public school personnel take place and joint projects are conducted.

- Collaboratively developed and executed in-service activities and joint research projects.

    Proposed new initiatives that will be undertaken if sufficient state funding materializes include the following:

- Programs for new teacher retention that provide university and mentor teacher supervision and support of first-year teachers.
- Programs, which began at the high school level, to attract minority students into teaching careers and provide incentives and support to prospective minority teachers.
- A center for development and study of effective educational practice and educational achievement in multicultural schools.

Avoiding Specious Symbols of Teacher Education Reform

    Higher education is not immune to self-serving notions. We also succumb to using committees and task forces to impose our personal dreams and add to our own professional esteem and self-importance. Any far-ranging recommendation to improve the education of teachers must be able to withstand a crucial test. Will it contribute to the well-being and improvement of the teacher or merely serve as parochial self-interest? Will the proposed recommendation stand a reasonable chance of improving classroom instruction and thereby achieve the educational goals we have for our children? One proposal that has been receiving attention around the nation is the concept of a teacher examination. In fact, such examinations have been imposed by legislatures in Texas, Florida, Oklahoma, and Alabama. In 1984 eighteen states required a paper-and-pencil test for certification, and thirty states had plans to introduce, or institute, additional means of assessment by 1987. The concept of a teacher examination is a seductive one, implying as it does a quantitative measure of quality and suggesting an impartial way to decide who has attained this level of quality and who has not. In fact, everyone in higher education should question, indeed vigorously oppose, the tendency of legislative bodies and even teachers' unions to adopt paper-and-pencil "teacher exams" as a gating mechanism for entering the field. In essence, we in higher education would hand off our responsibility for the curriculum and for professional preparation to a separate bureaucracy by supporting a teacher's examination.

Colleagues in the legal profession would be the first to admit that the bar examination administered in various states, even though prepared and in large part administered and evaluated by lawyers, does little to lift or maintain the quality of the law profession. It does not ensure qualified practitioners, and it is in no way the mechanism by which prestigious law firms choose the best lawyers to serve with them. It serves only as a minimum entry mechanism at the state level. In addition, a distressing private industry for tutoring people for the bar examination has grown up around it. The most promising lawyers, who obtain the best positions, are those who—in the opinion of their law school professors—have performed very well. This selection model, based on in-depth observations, is the one that I believe we should adopt for aspiring teachers. Prospects should be carefully chosen by our faculties for admission to preprofessional training; they should be educated with rigor; and, after they have completed their formal courses of study, they should be certified—again on the advice of our faculties—as competent to enter the profession.

The next few years are a critical period for us in teacher education; we must seize the initiative in improving our curricular offerings and encouraging capable students to choose the teaching profession. In the nation's view, if we fail to do this, we will deserve to have other organizations preempt our responsibility to determine the preparation needed and to make the determination that an individual is fit to teach effectively in the classroom.

Tests for assessment during the preservice educational period, especially when used to help the student analyze his or her own strengths and weaknesses, should be periodically administered. However, our ability is indeed limited to test solely in writing for interpersonal skills, empathy with children, commitment to teaching as a profession, and numerous other behav-

ioral components of the teacher. Those important assessments
are better done collectively by faculty who know teacher candidates well after lengthy classroom and student teaching experience with them.

The President and Accreditation

At a recent Wingspread Conference on Teacher Education, sponsored by the American Association of State Colleges
and Universities, the university presidents in attendance agreed,
wholeheartedly and passionately, that one of the major issues
affecting their successful management of the campuses' academic enterprise was that of accreditation. Regional accrediting
associations across the country have differing standards and perspectives regarding the meaning of the baccalaureate degree.
Campus regional accreditation reviews are often not substantive
and do not always focus on critical educational issues.

One area of continuing concern to our campuses is the
endless proliferation of specialized accrediting associations. The
Council on Postsecondary Accreditation (COPA) recognizes almost forty specialized accrediting agencies, one of which ac-
credits no fewer than sixteen separate programs in the allied
health area. The initial premise for such specialized accreditation was the establishment of agreed-upon educational standards on a nationwide basis in fields related to the health and
safety of the public. However, the growth in numbers of such
agencies has led to extensive duplication of effort, in that enormous amounts of faculty and administrative time are spent in
preparing self-studies, hosting accrediting teams, and responding
to their reports. The process is expensive; worst of all, partly because of the uneven and often excessively quantitative standards
put forward by the specialized accrediting associations, it does
not always ensure that the academic programs under review are
of high quality.

Nevertheless, when planned well and executed properly,
accreditation of programs by a team of one's peers is the best
method we have to ensure programmatic excellence. Here, university presidents can and should play a pivotal role. Just as

presidents have moved back into a determining position for the rules that govern athletics on our campuses, they must become very interested and vocal and serve actively on the bodies involved with accreditation.

For teacher education programs, a good regional accreditation process ideally would ensure that the overall academic setting is appropriate for educating the teacher. Next, the National Council for Accreditation of Teacher Education (NCATE) must have our support and involvement, so that it can function effectively. The NCATE process encourages institutions to meet rigorous academic standards defined by the practicing and preparation leaders of the profession. Through this process of professional accreditation, which relies on standards based on research and recognized professional best practice, the quality and academic integrity of programs are strengthened. Most important—in contrast to state program approval procedures, which often take the form of a compliance review of minimum standards—professional accreditation focuses on criteria for excellence and the dynamics needed for continuing program development. While in 1983 only 40 percent of the institutions preparing teachers were nationally accredited, about 80 percent of the largest public institutions were NCATE accredited. NCATE accreditation can increase the credibility of teacher education programs, sometimes sadly lacking, in the eyes of the public, profession, and the policy makers.

Other professions have successfully used a good accreditation process to ensure the quality and rigor of their programs. Programs in engineering, for example, and residency programs in medicine are managed by outstanding professionals in the field and enjoy the respect of the faculty and institutions undergoing accreditation. A rigorous accreditation process concentrates on the extent to which a program's goals in preparing students to become professionals are achieved. It does *not* concentrate on faculty salary and office size, the absolute numbers of volumes in the library, or the faculty's research productivity unless research is directly related to the program undergoing review. Responsible program review also needs to have some teeth in it. Putting a program on probation or withhold-

ing approval should have important meaning for that program
and for the campus.

Improving Programs for Elementary School Teachers

Like Jacob, who toiled seven years and then another seven
for his ultimate reward of marrying Rachel, the elementary
school teacher has toiled honorably and generally unnoticed
over the last couple of decades. Yet most institutions have developed a strong curriculum in elementary education. The advances made in knowledge about early childhood education, the
teaching of reading and mathematical concepts, nurturing creativity in children, and the teaching of children with learning
difficulties and neurological abnormalities have been quietly
and unassumedly revolutionary in their impact. This lack of attention to the elementary teacher is an interesting phenomenon
in the 1980s, a time when academic review groups have scruti-
nized every aspect of our nationwide educational system except
perhaps the cafeteria. Three recent studies by prestigious commissions (National Commission for Excellence in Teacher Education, 1985; California Commission on the Teaching Profession,
1985; Carnegie Task Force on Teaching as a Profession, 1986)
focus almost entirely on the teacher preparing to teach high
school and, in a limited fashion, the middle school. Few studies
that recognize the educational needs of prospective elementary
school teachers reach the higher education community or the
lay public. Most newspaper and other media coverage predict-
ing doom for the public schools focus on the high school teacher.

When we consider that approximately two-thirds of the
teachers needed in the next twenty years will be elementary
school teachers, the lack of attention to this group becomes
even more striking. The special knowledge required to teach the
small child, an extensive practical grasp of developmental psychology, the understanding of curriculum, and the depth of
knowledge in the various elementary school curricula comprise
a broad and very solid undergraduate curriculum. In contrast to
the raging national struggles over the level of achievement a student should have in physics or the social sciences before being

admitted to pedagogical courses, most institutions have quietly, deliberately, and with intellectual scrutiny developed a strong elementary education curriculum. However, our teacher training programs for elementary school teachers still can be improved. The suggestions by Miller and Mindess (1985) are excellent— especially their recommendations that prospective elementary teachers be given classroom experience early in the preparation program and that pedagogical methodology be rigorously taught.

Presidential Responsibility for Teacher Preparation

To paraphrase the famous verse from Ecclesiastes, "the time for teacher education" is very much at hand. If presidents, academic administrators, deans of colleges of education, and the entire university faculty will only seize this opportunity, a rich and rewarding revitalization of teacher preparation will occur. If we do not seize the initiative on our campuses at this time, the alternatives are clear. There will be increasing legislation, and increasing numbers of state agencies will regulate teacher credentialing. Worst of all, the profession will not prosper and gain its needed and deserved status. Outstanding education results when a well-prepared teacher works with children who are ready and eager to learn. We in higher education can do something about recruiting and developing the well-prepared teacher. This responsibility clearly rests with us.

10   *Linda Bunnell Jones*

Building Campus-Wide Support for Teacher Education

Today many leaders in teacher education appear to doubt that their faculty colleagues in departments preparing students to teach particular subjects have either the interest or the will to address the special needs of prospective teachers. And they propose a sequence of first a baccalaureate degree and then formal teacher preparation at the graduate level, in imitation of the professional school model of law, medicine, and the clergy. Some leaders in arts and sciences are just as doubtful about their ability to meet the needs of prospective teachers within the baccalaureate. They fear that a "watered-down" curriculum will be created, in which separate but not equal courses in specific disciplines are offered prospective teachers. Better to offer the same preparation in English or mathematics to the prospective teacher, they say, as to the prospective Ph.D. candidate. No compromise in rigor or quality can be charged in such an arrangement, they argue. But the best education for a teacher demands that the university encourage both faculties to relate formal instruction in teacher education to preparation in the subjects to be taught.

The education of a teacher requires a melding of subject-matter knowledge and instructional methods appropriate to grade levels. Such a sequential approach as that dictated by a postbaccalaureate teacher education program subverts the integration of content and form that is essential to the preparation of the beginning teacher.

Those universities for whom teacher education is a central mission can, through collaboration among and between deans and department heads, establish teacher education as a campus-wide responsibility. Powerful leadership from academic vice presidents will be required. With the institution of appropriate fiscal and personnel policies, new approaches to governance of teacher education, and closer collaboration between the public school teachers and campus faculty, deans and department heads can lead faculties to a shared commitment to teacher preparation.

Proposals to establish the education of teachers at the core of the university are not new, and their record of success is not good. Nevertheless, recent external pressure—in the form of public concern over the decline in student performance in America's schools when compared with that of other nations', as well as concern over prospective teachers' poor performance on basic skills tests—is causing universities to take a more comprehensive, collegial view of the education of teachers. And renewed interest of university faculty in the success of our public schools is lending internal support to such changing perspectives. A barrier to campus-wide responsibility remains the low regard in which teacher education programs and teacher education students are held on many campuses. Deep skepticism remains about the place of formal teacher education in the university—that is, discrete university courses designed to offer practical assistance to prospective teachers. Having not had formal preparation to teach themselves, faculty in the arts and science departments at major research institutions and at universities that have made a transition from normal schools to multipurpose institutions in the last thirty-five years tend to place little value on such a curriculum. In some instances, only the requirements of state licensing agencies have preserved formal teacher education in the university curriculum. State policies for credentialing, however, tend to isolate professional teacher education. And because such requirements are driven by external forces, rather than by the entire university faculty's belief in the merit of such work, professional education courses and the students who opt for them have typically been seen as second rate.

Impetus for the All-University Approach

In 1963 James Conant, then president of Harvard University, recognizing how detrimental such a perspective was to the education of prospective teachers, called for teacher education to become an all-university responsibility. Specifically, the university president—on behalf of the entire faculty—should certify that the prospective teacher had completed courses in key academic subjects and was adequately prepared to teach in a specific field. In addition, the university's trustees should insist on continuing effective all-university or interdepartmental approaches to the education of teachers.

Conant's recommendations were in direct response to the doubts expressed in the late 1950s, following the Soviet Union's successful *Sputnik* launching in 1957, about the quality of America's secondary school education. The public then perceived that America's schools had not sufficiently prepared students in mathematics and science, so that they could be competitive engineers and designers of the explorations of outer space. As Paul Woodring (1975) observed, public concern over students' command of basic subjects prompts attention to the education of their teachers in the subjects they are to teach.

A similar question about America's international competitive edge arose in the early 1980s. This time it was stimulated by rapid economic and technological advances in Japan and other nations. Declining scores of American students on both the verbal and the mathematics portions of the Scholastic Aptitude Test led to cries of "Back to Basics" and to questions about teachers' command of basic skills. Legislators in over half of the states implemented tests of basic skills for prospective teachers. An alarming number failed to pass. This demonstrated lack of teachers' preparation in basic subjects has spread doubt about the depth of preparation in the subjects to be taught.

The Quick Fix

As a quick-fix solution to the problem of ensuring teachers' preparation in subjects to be taught, many people believe that prospective teachers should be required to pass standardized paper-and-pencil tests of subject-matter knowledge, either for admission to a teacher education program or for earning a teaching credential. The effort here appears to be to assign responsibility to the arts and science faculty, who—in the opinion of legislators and others—now appear to ignore it. The assumption is that they will be motivated by embarrassment over the poor performance of students to revise curricula or impose higher standards.

Teacher testing appeals to those who want political support to improve the status of the teaching profession in fiscal and social terms. Teacher organizations, school boards, and school administrators want prospective employees to be well screened, preferably by others. Schools of education often support testing as well, out of a desire to upgrade the status of the teaching profession and with the hope that schools of education then could, especially if teacher education is a postbaccalaureate program, be accorded the same respect that schools of medicine and law enjoy. Testing appeals to some faculty in the arts and sciences because it appears to transfer the burden for preparation of teachers to the students themselves. Arts and science faculty are then free to emphasize the education of specialists in the discipline, at the expense of an approach more responsive to the needs of the public schools.

While standardized testing for entrance to the profession may be acceptable in medicine or law, it is not for the teaching profession. The differences in fiscal reward, client relationship, length of induction period, selectivity in admissions, not to mention the differences in the sheer number and variety of teachers needed in comparison to lawyers and doctors, dictate a different approach to the education of teachers. Universities must seek to *enable* students to become effective teachers. Form and content, learning what is to be taught in conjunction with how to teach it, must be brought together to create the best teacher. The student must not be left alone to relate formal instruction in the psychology and sociology of human learning to instruction in, for example, history or literature.

Leadership to Effect Campus-Wide Responsibility

Central executive and academic leadership will be required to bring departments and schools offering majors in the arts and sciences together with those offering formal instruction in teaching. The campus president can and must use his office as a "bully pulpit," calling for faculty who extend and expand basic skills, who provide education in breadth and depth, and who instruct in the practice of teaching to accept their mutual responsibilities for the education of teachers. The president must him- or herself, through a visible and meaningful working relationship with local school superintendents, demonstrate the necessity of an alliance between the university and the public school.

But meaningful extracampus collaboration with the schools and intercollaboration between the arts and science faculty and schools of education will depend on an academic leader with the mandate to bring together arts, sciences, and education faculty to make decisions about teacher education and with the power to allocate resources to reflect a policy of overall campus responsibility for teacher education. On most campuses the vice president or associate vice president for academic affairs serves this function.

Critical to a campus-wide acceptance of responsibility for teacher education is a faculty and administrative governance structure that can allow the concept to win widespread support and can provide sound recommendations to the vice president about implementation of policy. A Council for Teacher Education should be established, with department heads and faculty from arts and sciences and education and the deans of those schools as members and with the vice president as chair. The council's first order of business should be to determine whether the responsibility for teacher education is already shared across the campus. This process of self-study is a valuable tool for involving all faculty, for raising consciousness, and for identifying areas where improvement is needed in collaboration or where new opportunities for collaboration might be explored. Areas that should be studied include policies on faculty hiring, assignment of faculty to methods courses and to supervise student teachers, faculty research and community service, selection of students for admission to teacher education and for recommendation for a credential, advising of prospective teachers, and collaboration in curriculum development in arts and sciences based on familiarity with the public school curriculum.

Personnel Policies in Support of Campus-Wide Responsibility

Policies for hiring, retention, and assignment of faculty are at the heart of a genuine campus-wide concept of the education of teachers. The Council for Teacher Education should consider recommendations that support the significant involvement of the larger numbers of faculty in teacher education. The most obvious means to ensure a close connection between the arts and science departments and the school of education is a policy requiring faculty in teacher education to hold appointments in both units. Joint appointments might be made between teacher education and psychology, sociology, or political science—disciplines that have direct applications in teacher education programs. Joint appointments between disciplines commonly taught in the schools and teacher education programs may be even more vital. Such faculty can teach methods courses in the school of education, and they can also communicate their department's overall perspective on the preparation of teachers.

Objections are typically raised to joint appointments on the grounds that they are unfair to the individuals holding them. Critics say that each department may seek full allegiance from the appointee, with the result that superhuman performance is required to achieve tenure, or else the appointee may tend to place more energy in one unit, with the result that the other unit declines to award tenure. Although such obstacles should not be minimized, they can be overcome. A carefully conducted search enjoying full participation of both department heads, careful agreements about the appointees' obligations to each unit, and clear understanding about criteria for tenure are essential. These last should be reviewed by the vice president to ensure that they are commensurate with requirements imposed by single-department appointments.

Where joint appointments are not feasible, teaching loads may be divided between departments as two-thirds/one-third. Or—especially on campuses where a high percentage of faculty are tenured and few vacancies exist—a faculty member from the arts and sciences might be given a two- to three-year appointment in the school of education, and vice versa. Finally, team teaching—a traditional means of bringing faculty with differing expertise together—might be considered. An obvious choice for this sharing of expertise is methods courses. Faculty in mathematics working closely with faculty in teacher education can develop genuine articulation between formal preparation in the mathematics department and applications to teaching it at various grade levels.

Even more desirable are shared responsibilities between arts and science faculty and teacher education faculty for supervision of student teachers. While the emphasis in student teaching has traditionally been on the practice of formal teaching techniques, new demands that prospective teachers should focus on the subject they intend to teach call for the presence of faculty from the various subject areas. Supervision by faculty who hold appointments in the arts and sciences and by teacher education faculty is the solution to providing combined expertise.

Team teaching of courses and supervision teams are more costly in resources, but they provide the direction needed by prospective teachers; at the same time, they give faculty in the arts and sciences a better understanding of formal instruction in teaching and a knowledge of classroom applications.

Since the supervision of student teachers is highly expensive, available resources often are not adequate for one faculty supervisor to carry out these duties, let alone two. In many institutions faculty supervise student teachers at a ratio of 1 to 25. In other words, supervision of twenty-five prospective teachers would constitute a full-time teaching load for one faculty member for one term. An assignment of twenty-five students *might* be mangeable in a laboratory situation, but it is hardly practicable when students are placed in many different schools. A ratio reduced to 1 to 15 would permit a faculty member in English, for example, to supervise three to four students in lieu of teaching a single course (in a total load of three or four courses).

A less costly approach is that of the subject "coach," a faculty member in arts and sciences who does not bear primary responsibility for supervision but who visits the student teacher several times to observe integrity of subject-matter presentation and to whom the student can turn for assistance in developing or implementing a course of study. Faculty in arts and sciences might be paid an overload for this modest level of supervision or take on such responsibilities in lieu of other service commitments on the campus or in the community. Even so modest an approach as that of serving as "coach" makes faculty in arts and sciences better acquainted with the curricula in their field at various grade levels in the schools and therefore more able to help prospective teachers acquire skills and knowledge in the major or in general education courses.

Admission to Teacher Education Programs

In addition to recommending policies for broadening faculty participation in teacher education, the Council for Teacher Education should develop admissions policies that promote a thorough evaluation of prospective teachers by arts and science faculty *and* teacher education faculty. Evaluation of basic skills must be carried out by faculty specialists in writing, mathematics, and oral communications. Most critical, of course, is evaluation by the arts and science faculty of the students' command of the subjects to be taught. Course grades are the crudest measure. Requiring students to earn passing or more than passing grades in courses that are foundations for teaching the school curricula is a step toward coherence in preparation. For example, all prospective secondary English teachers should take advanced composition courses. Well-developed writing courses will help them teach others to write.

To test a student's grasp of essential concepts, departmentally developed comprehensive examinations or oral examinations should call on the student to explain basic premises of the structure and methodology of the discipline as well as to demonstrate basic grasp of information. On the basis of these assessments, the department could recommend additional work or immediate admission to the teacher education program. Such evaluation is far more difficult for elementary teachers, who must present knowledge of many fields; but faculty in key disciplines can collaborate in evaluating the broad knowledge of these students.

Teacher education faculty need to evaluate applicants as well. Some demonstration of likelihood of success in teaching should be required of students prior to admission to a teacher education program. Far too many students are well into completion of a credential before they realize that they do not really like to teach and do not have the skills to succeed. Requiring an early field experience in a school, with observation by university teacher education faculty, would go far to screen out those who are not suited to teaching and to select those who are.

Academic Advising Policies

Too often students seek academic advising only as they enter the teacher education program. By then they may have lost the opportunity to make course selections that would contribute to their preparation to teach. The Council for Teacher Education should institute a strong prospective teacher orientation and advisement program that relies heavily on participation by arts and science faculty. If a campus has a central advising center, all advisers should be prepared to give good direction on course selection to those students with undeclared majors or those majoring in arts and sciences who might consider teaching. Since many arts and science majors choose teaching as an afterthought, almost all these students should become familiar with the basic requirements for solid teacher preparation.

A common practice designed to ensure coherence in course selection or the selection of a major is the designation of a single departmental adviser for prospective teachers. The status of such a person within the department is critical. If, for example, the department head or another highly respected faculty member is selected, the status of being a prospective teacher is enhanced in the minds of students and faculty. The departmental adviser needs to be in close contact with the school of education and aware of public school curriculum in the discipline. Literature about credential requirements should be available in the department and a recommended selection of courses published, in consultation with teacher education faculty and local teachers. In addition, students preparing to be teachers could be brought together in informal meetings or even departmental clubs.

Departmental advisers also should be involved in the screening of prospective teachers. They should provide students with honest information about the advantages and disadvantages of a teaching career; and they should encourage students whose communication skills seem deficient, or who are otherwise unsuited to teaching, to consider other career choices long before decisions are made about formal application to teacher education.

Finally, departmental advisers should play an important role in making recommendations of students to teacher education. They should be able to identify strengths and weaknesses, comparing and even ranking students for admission to teacher education.

Collaboration in Departmental Curriculum Development

Prospective teachers should be expected to range widely in course selection. The history major who takes most of his courses in Asian history will face extensive background preparation when he finds himself assigned to teach five high school classes in American history. At the same time, each prospective teacher should explore a specialized subject in depth, so as to be able to provide students with the experience and pleasure of mastering a narrowly defined area of study.

Breadth and depth should be the guiding principles of course selection, with attention to subjects that prospective teachers are most likely to be expected to teach in the schools. Children's literature is an obvious choice for elementary teachers; but so is American literature, since much of the public school curriculum in literature is drawn from that area. In an English course on the history of the novel, for example, students can be encouraged to select from those American classics that are often read in the schools. In addition, adjunct courses might be offered for prospective teachers. A one-unit course could be offered, for example, as an adjunct to the standard Shakespeare course, to give students a feeling for ways in which pupils at elementary or secondary levels could be introduced to themes and ideas in the plays.

In order to develop emphases within existing courses or to develop adjunct courses, faculty in the arts and science departments may need to work with faculty in the school of education and to get ideas from teachers and curriculum designers in the local schools. A few campuses have invited exemplary teachers from local high schools to spend a year on campus, teaching in an arts and science department and working closely with prospective teachers.

Faculty Research, Consultation, and Community Service

Better knowledge on the part of arts and science faculty of the public school curriculum at various grade levels would surely enhance their instruction of prospective teachers and their ability to develop a meaningful curriculum in departmental offerings. The recent concern over student preparation has motivated many faculty members to become interested in the quality of the public schools. In California, postsecondary faculty are attempting to determine how much entering students need to know about key academic subjects in order to succeed in college. As a result, many have become actively involved in school improvement and partnership projects. Still, there are too few opportunities, let alone incentives, for arts and science faculty to become involved in meaningful ways that promote genuine understanding of the school curriculum.

In addition to the more obvious structural approaches, such as supervision or coaching of student teachers by arts and science faculty, the Council for Teacher Education should recommend that faculty members undertake research and consultation projects in the public schools in subject-specific areas. For example, a study by history faculty of high school students' understanding of American history could lead to findings to guide textbook development as well as university preparation. And up-to-date scientists can review science instruction in the schools, to make sure that it reflects the latest research.

School districts bear their share of responsibility for encouraging and structuring this research on the part of faculty in arts and sciences. Too often, when consulting services or advice is sought, the tendency is not to look beyond the faculty in teacher education. A campus-designated liaison for contact with the public schools could be selected to identify faculty interested in such research or consultation and to broker these services to the schools.

In addition, recognition of service to the schools in the promotion and tenure process should be encouraged. Service or research connected with the public schools often is regarded on campus as less "respectable" than highly specialized research or professional activity in the discipline at the university level. A central problem is documentation of such work so as to enable faculty committees to evaluate its value and impact. Of course, published work reviewed by peers is the best means of demonstrating the results of such research or consulting. But the Council for Teacher Education needs to explore, even establish, other forums for demonstrating the skill and knowledge required and its impact on schools; and guidelines should be created for its measurement.

Implementation of Recommendations

Once the Council for Teacher Education has made its recommendations, the vice president needs to create a mechanism for keeping the focus on campus-wide responsibility. The council should stay active to oversee and lead faculty to implement changes. But no committee can long remain in charge of a program, and no vice president for academic affairs can long focus attention on a single aspect of the university program, no matter how important. Perhaps the wisest approach to campus-wide responsibility for teacher education is a new, broader concept of the role of dean or director of the school of education. He or she should not only preside over the professional education faculty but should also be responsible for integrating the arts and science faculty and the teacher education faculty. With such responsibility must go the power to provide incentives, to make decisions about who among the arts and science faculty will participate directly in teacher education and who will not. Given the heavy responsibility for contact with local schools already placed on deans and directors of education, senior administrators must recognize the need for additional support positions to provide liaison with the public schools.

Bringing about the changes recommended in this chapter will require leadership and vision on the part of university presidents, deans, department heads, principals, teachers, and faculty leaders, as well as the cooperation of school superintendents. The exact shape and form of these changes will differ from campus to campus, but at their heart is a commitment to excellence in education and a recognition of the teacher as a valued member of society.

11

John W. Porter

Enhancing the Status
of the Teaching Profession

Higher education in the United States is entering a period when its purposes and its quality are being questioned (Newman and Boyer, 1985). During the first part of the 1980s, the focus was on elementary and secondary schools. This focus culminated in the publication of *A Nation at Risk* (National Commission on Excellence in Education, 1983). Since then the American system of higher education, especially its role in preparing elementary and secondary teachers and in improving student performance in elementary and high school classrooms, has been subjected to public scrutiny.

During the first hundred years of the certification of teachers by normal schools and teacher colleges, from 1855 to 1955, the assumption was that those who were interested in entering the profession would be able to perform satisfactorily once they were able to complete the collegiate requirements. Given this assumption, the colleges that produced the nation's teachers clearly understood their mission, and the teachers entering the classrooms were comfortable with their role in determining which students should continue their education. A grading system of *A, B, C, D,* and *F* was established. Tests were instituted, and the screening of students was an acceptable practice.

These conditions provided a compatible environment for teacher training institutions and for teachers. The relatively low pay was not a deterrent, possibly because women were a majority in the teaching force. Some of these women were second wage earners; for others, the work schedule was compatible with family responsibilities. The schools still close for two weeks at Christmas, a week at Easter, and most of June, July, and August, as they did when the society was agrarian.

In the mid-1950s, school personnel were confronted by several issues that seemed to emerge as more important than student performance to justify expenditures: large increases in enrollments; efforts to desegregate the public schools; and the emergence of state and federal government in standardizing school activities, as a result of increased funding and the advent of collective bargaining. All these issues helped to focus attention on staffing patterns and the reporting of activities, rather than on classroom performance.

During most of these historic twenty years (1955–1975), enrollments in teacher education were increasing. Serious introspection seldom takes place in periods of prosperity. Thus, it is not surprising that, when teacher enrollments began to decline significantly in the 1970s, there was little sympathy for teacher education within other departments, in which enrollment continued to increase. In short, there was no precedent on college campuses to close ranks in order to strengthen teacher education and alter its decline of prominence.

In the remainder of this chapter, the focus will be on the role that can and should be played by the college or university president, and policy makers of higher education institutions, to influence substantial improvements in the prominence of the teaching profession.

Institutional Responsiveness and Teacher Education

The president, governing board, and other individuals responsible for the direction of a higher education institution that prepares teachers have numerous challenges, but none is more important than responding to the needs of the teacher education program. From the public's point of view, colleges and universities are both providing a liberal education and preparing their graduates for business, engineering, and other professions quite effectively. Yet, in the view of this same public, they are much less successful in the training of teachers.

Institutions in Transition. Prior to World War II, the distinction between preparing to teach and preparing to enter another profession was not highlighted on most college campuses, principally for two reasons often forgotten in the post-*Sputnik* era: (1) teaching was generally regarded as a field of endeavor principally for women; and (2) teacher preparation took place primarily in "teachers colleges," so that other professional schools, which did not emphasize teacher preparation, were not in competition for students who were planning to be teachers. The "baby boom" that began during World War II, coupled with the enactment of the GI Bill, set the stage for a fundamental reordering in the transition from school to college and in who would seek to teach. More first-generation college-bound students began to show up on college campuses, and more men —primarily GIs—entered college to obtain teaching certificates.

The World War II and postwar baby boom required more classroom teachers, more faculties, and more buildings—and the result was that there were lower standards in all areas. During this same time, the colleges, formerly normal schools or teachers colleges, in response to the growing enrollments, were expanding their curricula to provide majors in fields other than teaching. These two conditions—the need to certify more teachers and the desire of teachers colleges to broaden their curricula —are in part responsible for the declining status of teacher education programs on many college campuses. The teachers colleges did turn out more teachers, anyone able to meet state certification requirements, but did not require a systematic and independent verification of the talent of those being recommended. Some of these colleges also diverted dollars being generated by increased enrollments in education to support other initiatives on campus. In many instances the college president had to be concerned with meeting enrollment demands rather than maintaining standards for the teaching profession, and it seemed that the only course was to respond to the growing demand for more services and greater opportunities. Institutional responsiveness was embodied in the belief that everything would be bigger and, it was hoped, better.

Time for Institutional Commitment. As college enrollments began to taper off in the late 1970s, and the demand for better teachers reached new heights of concern in the early 1980s, college presidents and governing boards were faced with a dilemma of significant proportions. That dilemma, briefly stated, was how the newly established regional university of the 1980s could attract and prepare better students to enter the field of teaching and at the same time maintain its commitment to preparing students for other professions.

On nearly every campus where the tradition has been teacher preparation, the president, governing board, and staff are delving into this issue in the hope that they will find an answer to this dilemma (Monat, 1985). Responding to needs to support the teacher education program will require (1) willingness to seek out the very best students, (2) establishment of higher admission standards and assurance that graduates of the education program are among the most able, (3) new methods of instruction to improve classroom performance for those students most in need of improvement, (4) salaries that are competitive on a twelve-month basis, and (5) new methods of financing the public schools. These changes are fundamental to long-lasting improvement in the status of the teaching profession, and several are within the jurisdiction of college and university leaders.

Enhancing the Teacher Education Program

New support for teacher education is emerging. Students are once again showing an interest in teacher education—although academically talented women and minorities, who once were restricted to teaching as a professional option, are now able to choose other occupations that offer greater financial rewards, more opportunity for advancement, and improved working conditions (Darling-Hammond, 1984). With this new interest in teacher education, now is the time to strengthen the standards for admission to and graduation from teacher education. College and university presidents should not allow the standards for enrolling in the teacher preparation programs to remain among the lowest on campus simply in order to increase enrollments of women and minorities, as well as other students. If that transpires, a unique opportunity to enhance the status of the teacher education program will have been lost again. It is the responsibility of the chief executive officer, with the support of the governing board, to establish standards for the preparation of teachers second to none on the college campus. Establishing such standards implies that the administration also will vigorously support three prerequisites that are essential to the creation of higher standards:

1. Colleges with substantial teacher education programs will need to do a better job of working with high schools and community colleges to identify and involve students in the teacher/learner process.
2. College administrations will need to earmark greater amounts for scholarships to attract academically talented students interested in teaching into the teacher education programs.
3. The president and governing board will need to be committed to upgrading the faculty and staff in the teacher preparation area.

As noted earlier, bold new actions, led by the president, will be necessary to enhance the teacher education program. Each action will require the full support and efforts of the president and the governing body.

Outreach to High Schools and Community Colleges. Very little will take place on campuses until the president clearly indicates that he or she regards the recruitment of future teachers as an institutional priority. The president should request a specific outreach proposal from the education staff. Such a proposal should specify students to be targeted, summer enrichment opportunities, and program opportunities to assess the

potential of each high school and community college partici-
pant.

The establishment of "future-teacher clubs" as a way of
identifying and attracting academically able students to the
teacher education program is one promising approach that
needs to be supported by the president. Such programs should
be attractive and closely associated with the college or university. Exciting summer programs and year-long activities similar
to the Future Farmers of America clubs need to be instituted,
and special financial aid should be provided so that talented minority students can attend such programs.

Program Standards of Excellence. On most college campuses, those who enter the teacher preparation program during
the junior year are regarded as less academically talented than
students in other fields. This myth is perpetuated by the general perception that students with a 2.0 (or *C*) grade point average will be admitted into most teacher education programs. Colleges and universities interested in enhancing the status of the
teacher education program need to set forth, for public review,
their actual standards and criteria for admission to teacher education programs, to demonstrate that these standards are comparable to those of other professional schools on the campus.

In instances where the standards for admission to teacher
education are lower than those imposed by other professional
schools, administrators may be reluctant to raise them, because
they assume that higher standards will force the college to lose
students. There is evidence, however, that raising the standards,
and providing additional incentives for students to stay in the
program, will, in fact, encourage more students to seek acceptance into the teacher education program. Therefore, the president should request that a position paper be prepared on implementing a program of standards of excellence that would include such items as (1) an increased grade point average, (2) a
basic studies competence examination, (3) demonstrated clinical and field experience, and (4) interpersonal relationship indi-
cators.

Ensuring the Graduate's Competence. The teacher education curriculum needs to be carefully evaluated by practitioners,

to determine that the enrolled students are given the best and most comprehensive preparation available. Students should receive clear-cut, regular written and clinical evaluations of their performance. Such evaluations should measure subject-matter competence, test administration, pedagogy, knowledge of educational and human growth and learning theories, and effective application of classroom management techniques. Students should also, if possible, be given a final examination prior to recommendation for state certification. Such an exit examination—a comprehensive test of teacher competencies—would substantially enhance the teacher education program.

Some colleges and universities have "guaranteed" the quality of their graduates to employers. Such a guarantee has merit if properly utilized. Certainly, a more vigorous and continuous follow-up of graduates who enter the teaching profession should take place. Each president who seeks to enhance the quality of the teacher preparation program should, in a letter to prospective employers, "affirm" the preparation of the program's graduates (Monat, 1985). Again, the president needs to assume a leadership role in bringing about the changes necessary to affirm the competencies of each graduate from the teacher education program. Much debate will ensue on campus in regard to the policy of "affirming" the competence of each graduate. Some will say that such a practice may place the institution in jeopardy. These are difficult issues to resolve, but they are at the heart of what is necessary to raise the status of the teacher education program on the campus.

In addition to these major commitments of energy and resources, smaller actions can also assist. A number of professional schools, for instance, have special ceremonies to recognize their graduates in addition to commencement. Thought should be given to such recognition for the graduates of the teacher education program. Special certificates could be presented, and the employers of the graduates invited to the special ceremonies.

The president can make a major difference in the institution's teacher education program by acknowledging that it deserves the full support of the total university resources. Only through such a commitment can there be any hope that the program will emerge to a more prominent place. In many respects enhancing the status of the teacher education program is no different from efforts to improve any academic program or athletic team. *Improvement of any program or team takes better teaching and more talented recruits.* Both better teaching and more talented recruits usually require that more money be invested in the enterprise. The teacher education program can gain prominence in academia, but only if the leadership on campus is willing to press for the changes and the resources that have been proposed.

Changing the Public Perception of the Teacher

The saying "Those who can, do; those who can't, teach" is more than a catchy slogan. It says a lot about the attitude of the American public. Most of the continuing controversy about "why Johnny can't read" has focused on poor teaching. Teachers are on the defensive because of parent permissiveness, student apathy, overbearing and unimaginative administrations, and a lack of public prominence (Michaels, 1985). Getting the public to recognize and reward the outstanding work of teachers would provide the needed momentum for building the status of the teaching profession.

Only within the past three decades, since 1954, have America's teachers been asked to perform in an environment for which they were not well prepared. During most of our first two centuries as a nation, the teacher's responsibility was to challenge the students enrolled and to select those who should be encouraged to continue their studies. For the others there were hired-hand jobs on the farm and blue-collar jobs in the factories. Desegregating the schools was not an issue, and television had not yet invaded the family living room.

Within a very short time following World War II, the teacher's role was dramatically transformed.

Teachers were confronted with competition from television, which makes today's student expect to be entertained.

Teachers were faced with the new national policy that all students should be able to succeed in school.

Teachers joined unions to protect their interests and began to voice their concerns as a group rather than as individuals.

Teachers as a group began to demand greater salaries, more benefits, and different working conditions.

Teachers as a group increased dramatically in number and changed in composition after World War II, and the result was a philosophical change in the attitudes of many of those in the profession.

These changes—all of which occurred between 1955 and 1975—were not well received by all of the American public. Taxes were increasing, schools were being desegregated, students were being bussed, both parents were working, and the school as the bedrock of the community was rapidly losing its constituency. There are no signs on the horizon that these forces, which brought about a decline in the prestige and prominence of the classroom teacher, are waning. In many respects they may even be increasing.

Moreover, the new national policy brought about conflicting expectations of the teacher. On the one hand, the public expects the teacher to determine the progress of each student; and when a student is not performing, the teacher is expected to grade the student accordingly. On the other hand, national policy since 1955 has been translated as meaning that no student can be labeled a failure.

These contradictory expectations have created much of the public's negative attitude and are at the heart of the crisis in the American classroom (Hulik, 1985). The schools did not reorganize to respond to the new national policy, and the public did not accept it.

Teachers need to be free of the constraints of overbearing administrators and public pressures to water down the curriculum. If local, state, and national officials would adopt a pact to relieve the teacher of the responsibility for ensuring that every student succeeds, the image of the teacher could be dramatically improved within a decade. The university can play an important

role in this regard by developing a failure safety net that re-
cycles students who are not able to maintain academic progress.

The problems that have resulted in the declined status of
the teaching profession in the public's eye are easily identified
and will need to be corrected, in fact as well as in perception, if
the level of prominence of the teaching profession is to be significantly raised. Those problems are:

1. Post-World War II enrollments, which resulted in perceived
    lower teacher preparation standards.
2. A perceived deemphasis on the quality of the teacher's
    preparation.
3. Across-the-board salary increases.
4. Emphasis on equal educational opportunities, which re-
    sulted in a belief that all students must succeed within a set
    time frame.
5. Corporation competition for the better college graduates,
    which resulted in a salary differential between business and
    education and thereby made teaching less attractive.
6. Increased social demands, which resulted in more competi-
    tion to attract the attention of women and minority stu-
    dents.

These six problem areas stand as a guarded fortress to any attempts to change public perception of teachers.

Changing the public's perception of the teaching profession also will require diminishing the discrepancy between what
college students and teachers think are low annual salaries, poor
working conditions, and lack of respect, and what taxpayers believe are high per hour costs for employing teachers, poor performance, and lack of professionalism.

Starting salaries for teachers are clearly far behind the annual starting salaries in various businesses. That is why a majority of students are now enrolling to obtain degrees in business
administration. However, when the hours of classroom contact
are compared to the number of hours of business contact, the
starting salaries for teachers are competitive. Noneducators, on
the other hand, do not consider the number of noncontact

hours that teachers must spend in their work. College and university presidents can help ameliorate the discrepancy in public and teaching profession perceptions of effort expended in relation to pay received.

Changing the public's perception of the teaching profession will necessitate creating an environment, however, where the teacher is employed for a full year and paid on a comparable scale. The idea of nine months of teaching—or 180 days of class contact—is based on an agrarian society, which no longer exists. A twelve-month, full-time employment schedule (with reduced compensation provided for those teachers who request a reduced schedule of employment) does not necessarily translate into assuming that the students will be in school for twelve months. To bring teacher salaries up to the standard of others with comparable education and responsibilities, on a twelve-month basis, could involve assignments in summer teaching or in course planning and development or redevelopment, or even exchange arrangements with businesses or higher education. In addition to the increased pay, such experiences could also be beneficial to the teacher's further professional development.

If the colleges raise standards, and attract top faculty and students to the teacher education program, the first steps will have been taken. If teachers can be placed on a full-year schedule and paid twelve-month salaries, the foundation for enhancing the status of the teaching profession will have been established, and a significant change in public perception will begin to take place. The remaining ingredient to change public perception is what actually happens in the classrooms of American schools. To increase respect for the teaching profession, a significant improvement in student performance will be required in the lower half of the normal distribution curve.

Restructuring the Teaching Profession

In January 1986 Christa McAuliffe, a Concord, New Hampshire, high school teacher, was scheduled to turn the space shuttle *Challenger* into an orbiting classroom, which would have been viewed on television by millions around the world. By her presence aboard the shuttle and her boundless enthusiasm, the educators and leaders of the nation had hoped to demonstrate the impact of teachers on our society. Christa McAuliffe had hoped to launch new energy into a profession increasingly plagued by poor salaries, "burnout," and a lack of respect (Fisher, 1985).

Astronaut McAuliffe believed that a good teacher has to capture the imagination of the students: "When you walk into the classroom, you're on stage front and center. Even at a quarter of eight in the morning, if the kids are not very responsive, the teacher needs to get them excited because that's what teaching is all about" (Fisher, 1985, p. 1).

The first teacher-astronaut never made it into space, but she left behind a wonderful legacy. For the first time in more than a quarter of a century, the two million teachers of America were seen in a new light. Suddenly our schools received more attention than they had ever been given before. Seven brave Americans died with the destruction of the *Challenger* on January 28, 1986, but it was the death of a teacher that made children across the nation cry and parents realize the value of the classroom. Christa McAuliffe's gift was not in the skies, but here on earth. She was an exceptional teacher before the scheduled flight, and she planned to continue teaching when she returned from space. In death, her legacy gave to her fellow professionals new dignity, honor, and a feeling of pride to say, "I am a teacher too."

This episode epitomizes the challenge that faces the American nation. Most Americans would like to be proud of their teachers, but everyone knows that not all teachers are equipped to be performers in an entertainment sense, excite the class every day, and instill the necessary skills into every student. American classrooms have generally been unable to utilize the technologies of television or computers in the past several decades to improve the attractiveness of the classroom. This fact—along with the unimaginative factory model of schooling, in which teachers are viewed as semiskilled and low-paid workers—makes the challenge of elevating the status of the teaching profession formidable.

Upgrading the quality of teacher preparation and creating more professional working conditions are part of a structural solution that attends to the interrelated causes of the problem as well as to the symptoms. In fact, teaching is now much like the legal and medical professions were at the turn of the century. Until fundamental changes were made in the structure of those professions, they too were characterized by low wages, easy access, poor training, no real standards of practice, and a poor public image (Darling-Hammond, 1984).

Reestablishing the Laboratory School. Studies conducted over the past several years show that students have different learning styles, require different amounts of time to learn, and need different settings. Appropriate teaching techniques must be determined by diagnosing students' needs and matching those diverse needs to appropriate methods of instruction. Exemplary applications of this information would be possible in the laboratory schools that at one time were associated with many teacher education programs. College and university presidents could help to bring about fundamental reform in education by collectively setting aside resources that would pilot new approaches to the educating of American young people, including putting together a new version of the laboratory school. No one institution can successfully influence the changes that are required. Only through long-term leadership of many colleges and universities can a program large enough be launched to significantly influence the present system and bring about the needed reforms.

Recommendations for Professionalizing Teaching. If the status of the teacher is to be significantly elevated, more than a few marginal changes in the attractiveness of the teaching profession will need to be made. Restructuring the teaching occupation will not be a simple undertaking. It will entail substantial costs, be politically difficult, and require profound organizational changes. However, with the assistance of courageous leadership from the colleges and universities, such changes can be accomplished (Newman and Boyer, 1985).

The first action is to establish professionally competitive salaries on a full-year basis for teachers: salaries beginning at

$25,000 and, with career increases based on performance, reaching $50,000 as measured by present conditions. This change may require the certification of paraprofessionals to work with teachers.

The second action is to allow experienced teachers to assume more responsibility for the success of their students. This responsibility should include curriculum development, instructional modification, and reporting student progress to a central data center for evaluation.

The third action is turn over to experienced teachers the responsibility for establishing the standards for entry into the profession, based upon a differentiated career ladder with specific evaluation and promotional points.

The fourth action is to provide recruitment incentives and attractive low-interest loans for academically talented college students to enter teaching. Such incentives should be so attractive as to offset offers that the private sector is able to provide.

The fifth action is to improve teacher education programs by making them more academically rigorous and requiring paid internships supervised by experienced teachers. Such internships would precede state certification. State tenure provision should be replaced by peer-defined standards of practice.

Although these five recommendations begin with higher salaries, they assume a major change in the working conditions within the schools and major shifts in resource allocations. The attention to education being generated by recent commission reports, the impending large-scale retirements, and the lack of any major social upheavals make these actions more feasible than ever before. The presidents of the universities that have a major responsibility for preparing our teachers should form a national compact to implement these proposals in existing local settings, thereby demonstrating the feasibility of the reforms. As noted by the Rand study, until teaching becomes a more attractive career alternative, the problems of attracting and retaining talented teachers will undermine the success of other reforms intended to upgrade educational programs and curricula (Darling-Hammond, 1984).

Conclusion

For nearly one hundred years, from 1850 to 1950, normal schools and teachers colleges provided the majority of the teachers, and these teachers served local communities with distinction and respect. However, during this period unionization did not exist, higher salaries were not a demand, desegregating the schools was not an issue, and the expansion of normal schools and teachers colleges was not at the forefront. The turbulence in the schools in the 1950s, the expansion of the 1960s, and the call for accountability in the 1970s provided a quarter of a century of turmoil and decline in the respect and prominence of the teaching profession.

In order to regain the prominence of teacher education and build the status of the teaching profession, three simultaneous actions are recommended:

First, increased numbers of qualified students must be attracted into the field of teaching to replace those who are nearing retirement from the expansive years between 1955 and 1975 (Runkel, 1985).

Second, if an equal educational opportunity is to be realized, the people recruited must be able to work with youngsters who need special attention.

Third, a program of greater credibility—which would, on any measure available or yet to be developed, confirm the quality of the program's rigor for the teacher education majors— must be developed on college campuses.

It is also here proposed that college and university presidents assume responsibility for helping to restore the prominence of teaching in American society.

12   *Richard C. Wallace, Jr.*

Establishing Partnerships Between Schools and Teacher Training Institutions

Why should teacher training institutions develop better relationships with the nation's schools? The reasons are multifold. First and foremost, it must be recognized that teacher development is a continuous process and that the responsibility for its progress must be shared among teacher training institutions, graduate schools of education, and local education agencies. Beginning teachers need time to acquire classroom management techniques and learn to orchestrate the myriad teaching tasks. Once they have mastered the mechanics of classroom management and instruction, they can begin to examine the effects that they are having on learners. Then, as teachers continue their development, they must acquire the sophisticated insights, through reflection and graduate studies, that will allow them to differentiate instruction for pupils. This process is well articulated in the publication *Teacher Development in Schools* (Academy for Educational Development, 1985).

Extensive dialogue among teacher preparation institutions, graduate schools of education, and the nation's schools is more necessary now than it has ever been in our educational history. All parties must clarify roles and responsibilities for preservice teacher training, graduate study, and continuing staff development in the schools. The scarcity of financial resources mandates such dialogue. If the challenge facing teacher education is to be met successfully, better ties must be established between local school districts and undergraduate and graduate educational institutions. A reexamination of the relationships among local education agencies and teacher training institutions also is imperative. The nation is demanding more effective performance of its schools. Enhanced performance in schools requires the use of effective instructional techniques by teachers and the use of instructional leadership skills by principals and support personnel. Teachers begin to develop and refine their teaching skills in teacher training institutions and then require several years of experience to achieve maturity. Teacher training institutions, graduate schools of education, and local education agencies must work closely together to identify appropriate roles for each in preservice, induction, in-service training, and continuing development of teachers. Effective working relationships among these institutions are required if teacher performance is to improve and if teaching is once again to become an attractive profession.

This chapter briefly describes a proposed undergraduate five-year teacher training program that involves an internship experience in the schools. The phases of teacher development then will be outlined, and various means of ensuring the continuing development of teachers will be explored. The final section of the chapter describes the Schenley High School and the Brookline Elementary School Teacher Centers in Pittsburgh, Pennsylvania, as examples of school-based professional development programs for teachers.

Undergraduate Teacher Education: A Five-Year Program

A five-year undergraduate program for the preparation of teachers should be implemented, along the lines of the Master of Arts in Teaching (M.A.T.) program (Academy for Educational Development, 1985) developed in the 1960s. In this program, which was designed to bring liberal arts graduates into the teaching profession, the teacher in training spent half of the fifth year in a paid teaching internship in the schools after completing a B.A. degree and a summer training program. The other half of the fifth year was spent in professional studies. The program culminated in an M.A.T. degree.

In the program proposed here, the first four years of teacher training would follow the conventional four-year liberal arts program, which would include some professional orientation experiences; and a paid fifth-year internship would help finance the student's additional year of training. The local education agency would assume complete responsibility for the internship supervision and would collaborate with a teacher training institution in facilitating the novice teacher's development. This type of arrangement would require close cooperation between the two institutions.

The academic portion of the fifth year of undergraduate teacher education should be school based in two ways. First, professional educational courses in pedagogy, testing, and child or adolescent psychology offered by the teacher training institution should be jointly taught by teacher educators and teachers in the schools. The faculty of teacher training institutions would be responsible for presenting theory and research, and the staff of local education agencies would demonstrate practical applications of theory and research. If possible, courses should actually be taught in schools, so that teachers in training could observe the application of the theory and research in classes with children and adolescents. Second, during the fifth year, the prospective teacher should be required to complete a thesis that combines research, theory, and practical application of some aspect of subject matter, pedagogy, or child/adolescent development. The thesis would force the prospective teacher to explore the complex interplay among research, theory, and practice and thereby develop an attitude of inquiry and reflection that is crucial to the long-term development of teachers in schools.

The fifth year of undergraduate teacher training must be preceded by carefully planned educational experience during the first four years of training. Among these experiences should be career awareness seminars, observations in schools, and personal assessment experiences that verify one's suitability for teaching. During this exploratory period, the prospective teacher should be assigned to a school-based teacher mentor, who would demonstrate teaching skills in the daily routine of teaching. Novices would observe and analyze the mentor's teaching techniques; tutor individuals or groups of students; coteach a lesson with the mentor; prepare instructional materials; prepare, administer, correct, and interpret tests; and the like. Upon completion of the five-year program, the student would be awarded a Bachelor of Arts degree and a provisional certificate for teaching and would be ready for induction into the profession.

Phases of Teacher Development

Although undergraduate teacher education and graduate studies in education are important aspects of a teacher's training, it must be acknowledged that competence in teaching is ultimately developed *in schools* over a long period of time. The Academy for Educational Development, in its 1985 report to the Ford Foundation, *Teacher Development in Schools*, highlights the growth process through which teachers must progress in order to attain maximum professional effectiveness. On the basis of two decades of experience in school improvement programs, the academy identifies four phases of teacher development: (1) career orientation and clinical training, (2) coping to understand and manage, (3) generalized pedagogy, and (4) differentiated pedagogy. The conditions required for growth throughout this development process include collegial support, feedback, and specific assistance.

The first phase of teacher development, career orientation and clinical training, occurs in schools, where prospective teachers gain experience and feedback in a clinical setting. The clinical training occurs during student teaching or internship experiences as the novice receives feedback on performance and begins to learn the relationships between theory and practice. During this first phase of teacher development, the schools and the teacher training institution work closely together.

The second phase, coping to understand and manage, occurs as the novice teacher takes on full responsibility as a first-year teacher. This phase of professional development is usually named induction. It essentially involves learning to survive in the classroom, the school, and the community. Classroom instructional management concerns tend to preoccupy teachers during induction. This focus on survival skills typically prevents the novice teacher from being able to perceive the sophisticated relationships among teacher strategies, curriculum themes, and student achievement. If a teacher is to develop beyond this coping phase, a supportive and stimulating environment will be required.

The third and fourth phases of teacher development, generalized and differentiated pedagogy, focus on the learning process of elementary and secondary students and on the need to diagnose and prescribe effective learning experiences for groups of students and individual students.

Promoting the Continuing Development of Teachers

In order to ensure the continuing development of teachers, as just described, local education agencies, teacher training institutions, and graduate schools of education must reexamine their respective roles and responsibilities. Teacher training institutions must provide undergraduate programs that reflect the latest research on teaching effectiveness. The schools must provide the supportive environment required to move teachers toward generalized and differentiated pedagogy. Graduate schools of education must provide teachers, supervisors, principals, and superintendents with a thorough understanding of effective instructional practices and must show school administrators how to promote the continuing development of teachers in schools. The relationships among school-based staff development programs and graduate programs in education must be much more clearly delineated if these programs are to be mutually supportive of each other.

Promoting Development During the Induction Process. The induction process takes place during the early stages of teacher development—that is, the first to third years of teaching. During these critical years, local education agencies must make teacher mentors available to novices. If new teachers are to develop their full potential, they must be exposed to good role models. They must work in schools where administrators and peers provide a supportive environment and constructive feedback. The profession needs to pay much greater attention to the induction process as an important component in the development of competence in the teaching profession. Teacher training institutions should collaborate with local education agencies to ensure effective induction of new teachers.

Role Relationships Among Teacher Training Institutions, Local Education Agencies, and Graduate Schools of Education. At this time it is not clear what precise roles each institution must play in bringing about the optimum conditions for teacher development in schools. The role of teacher training institutions in undergraduate teacher education must shift to providing a liberal arts program. If, as is suggested in this chapter, a fifth year of professional studies is added to the undergraduate program, that year should be devoted to a paid internship and professional studies that join theory, research, and practice. During this fifth year, the teacher training institution should take responsibility for presenting theory and research in such areas as child/adolescent growth, educational psychology, specific curriculum areas, and tests and measurement. The local education agency should provide the teacher trainee with practical application experiences related to the content of professional studies. Such an arrangement would require considerable cooperative planning among teacher training institutions and local education agencies. The local education agencies would have to provide skilled personnel to provide corrective feedback to teacher trainees. The supervision of the internship would have to be closely related to theory and research presented in the professional studies program at the teacher training institution. Teachers in local schools, who assume the role of "clinical teachers" and supervisors in the fifth year of the program, should be adjunct instructors in the teacher training institution. These adjunct instructors should collaborate with the institution's faculty in developing and implementing the professional studies offered in the fifth year of the teacher training program.

The role of graduate schools of education must also be re-examined with respect to the concept of teacher development in schools. Most graduate programs at the master's, certificate, or doctoral level tend to move students in a direction of specialization in a subject (such as English), a field of study (such as counseling or early childhood), or supervisory/administrative certification. Each of these areas of concentration should be examined in relation to teacher development in schools. Whereas skilled teacher behavior is acquired through practice, most graduate education programs tend to concentrate on knowledge transmission. Rarely are opportunities provided for graduate students to practice skills and receive feedback. Yet the research on adult education (Knowles, 1973) and staff development (Joyce and Showers, 1980) informs us that adults need to be active, not passive, learners and that skill development requires practice, feedback on practice, and coaching to application. These activities typically do not occur in most graduate education programs. They may not even occur in school-based staff development programs. Both oversights need to be corrected through collaborative planning.

If the development of teachers to their highest level of competence takes place in schools, the officials of teacher training institutions, graduate schools of education, and local education agencies must engage in extensive and continuous dialogue to ascertain each other's needs, interests, and resources. Failure to develop a well-articulated program of undergraduate, graduate, and in-service educational and staff development programs will tend to work against the promotion of professional competence in the schools and dissipate scarce financial resources.

Improving Teacher Performance in Pittsburgh

The Teacher Centers. The Schenley High School Teacher Center is the Pittsburgh School District's response to the board of education's mandate to increase the effectiveness of instruction in the secondary schools. The goal was to create a "model" secondary school for teaching and learning (Wallace and others, 1983). This model school would be designed to help secondary teachers in the school district improve their teaching skills and update their knowledge of their academic fields. Further, the school district suggested to the board that *all* secondary teachers in the district should be provided with a "mini-sabbatical" at this model school. The plan, developed by the district staff with representatives from the University of Pittsburgh, Duquesne University, and Carnegie-Mellon University, called for the board to restaff this school with the most able teachers in the district. The plan was approved by the board, and the Schenley High School Teacher Center was initiated in 1982. Intensive and detailed planning over the next year paved the way for the center's opening in August of 1983.

As mentioned, the primary purpose of the Schenley High School Teacher Center is to provide a teaching and learning experience for each secondary teacher in the Pittsburgh public schools. Teachers have an opportunity to (1) observe exemplary instructional activities in a real setting, (2) sharpen their current instructional skills by practicing new instructional techniques, (3) receive clinical feedback on that practice, (4) translate theory into practice, (5) receive an update in their specific subject-matter areas, (6) review the latest research findings in effective teaching, and (7) obtain a broad perspective of modern youth culture and its implication for effective teaching. A second purpose of the center is to provide an opportunity for teachers to engage in independent research activities, with a goal to create something that will be useful to them in their home school.

The general structure of the teacher's experience includes three phases: orientation, direct involvement, and reinforcement and support.

The first phase (orientation) is conducted by members of the Schenley High School Teacher Center staff in conjunction with visiting teachers, principals, and supervisors in the sending school. In this phase each teacher's needs are assessed; and an individualized study plan, reflecting the needs of both the individual teacher and the home school, is developed.

The second phase (direct involvement) takes place at

Schenley High School. Activities include but are not limited to the following:

1. Participation in seminars with peers and center staff, as well as university, business, and industrial personnel.
2. Involvement in clinical experiences, including observation of effective teaching, planning, actual teaching, and conferences.
3. Fulfillment of individual teacher plans, which may include working with university, community, and/or business resources.
4. Training in appropriate new technologies, including use of instructional media and computers.

The phase occurs over eight-week periods aligned with one of the four quarters of the school year. Specially trained replacement teachers teach the classes for the visiting teacher while he or she is at the center.

The third phase (reinforcement and support) occurs at the home school. The purpose of this phase of the program is to ensure retention and to support the teachers in the use of the skills and knowledge acquired at the center. This assistance will be a responsibility shared by the center's staff, the home school, and other staff, all of whom will have been appropriately trained.

The staff of the Schenley High School Teacher Center are among the best in the school district. The entire staff received intensive training and practice in the principles of effective instruction. Some resident teachers teach a reduced load of four classes and, in the remaining time, teach a series of seminars on adolescent development, orient teachers coming to the center, monitor research activities of peers, serve as models of exemplary teaching, and supervise the clinical component at the center.

One-third of the resident staff serve as clinical resident teachers. Each clinical resident teacher works with two visiting teachers in the "teaching clinic," which is based on the district's model of effective instruction. In this phase of the training, the visiting teachers assist in developing lesson plans, observe effective teaching, and have an opportunity to practice the model. The clinical teacher then provides them with structured feedback.

The on-site center is assisted by a cadre of forty-eight replacement teachers; these teachers are fully certified professionals whose teaching specialties represent the subjects offered at the secondary level. In the home schools, they replace those teachers who, for the period of eight weeks, are taking part in the center's program as visiting teachers.

The administration of the Schenley High School Teacher Center is a shared responsibility. The principal is responsible for all programs affecting the students and staff within the framework of the high school. The center's director is responsible for designing and implementing the program for visiting teachers.

The University of Pittsburgh's Center for International Studies staff worked closely with the Schenley faculty to develop and implement an international studies program for Schenley students. This four-year program culminates in the International Baccalaureate Diploma for those students who wish to pursue it. University faculty coteach some of the courses for Schenley students with Schenley faculty (for example, the course in theory of knowledge). Other university specialists lecture, periodically, on their area of expertise (for example, Central American foreign policy) to enrich the program for students. Both the university and school district personnel (including students) profit from this collaborative activity.

The Brookline Elementary School Teacher Center, modeled after the Schenley program, opened in August of 1985. The focus of the Brookline program is on instructional effectiveness, child development, and language acquisition in children. Brookline will serve as a development and demonstration center for new programs for Pittsburgh's elementary schools.

The primary focus of the Pittsburgh Teacher Centers has been on the revitalization of a veteran teaching staff in response to the board of education's mandate to improve student achievement and personnel evaluation. In the future the centers will serve as sites for orientation of new teachers. Closer cooperation with teacher training institutions in the training of prospective teachers will emerge as the district begins to hire new teachers in the 1990s. Because of enrollment decline and school closings, no new teachers were hired from 1979 to 1985.

Professionalizing the Role of Teachers in Pittsburgh. In August 1985 a new spirit of professionalism was achieved in Pittsburgh when the Pittsburgh Board of Education and the Pittsburgh Federation of Teachers reached an unprecedented agreement on a two-year contract extension one year prior to the expiration of the contract. The most notable part of the agreement was the stipulation that the parties engage in discussions regarding the professionalism of teachers. The primary goal of the federation is to enable teachers to participate in stimulating their own professional growth and that of their peers. The primary goal of the board of education is to enable teachers to participate in ensuring the quality of instruction and engage in effective planning and evaluation to promote effective student learning. Eleven committees of teachers and administrators are now discussing various issues related to these goals. A climate of trust and professionalism, which should promote continuing teacher development and enhanced student achievement, is developing in the city.

Summary and Implications

Better relationships between teacher training institutions and the nation's schools are needed because the development of the full potential of teachers actually takes place in the schools themselves. The central thesis of this chapter is that all agencies participate in the preparation and development of teacher competence; teacher training institutions, local education agencies, and graduate schools of education must coordinate their efforts and share in the responsibility for teacher development. These institutions must engage in much more active collaboration than has existed in order to plan their respective roles in the theory, research, and practice paradigm for teacher professional development.

Competent teachers in the public schools should serve as adjunct instructors in teacher training programs. Personnel in teacher training institutions should take the responsibility for presenting theory and research related to educational practice. Courses in pedagogy should take place in public school settings, where the practical application of theory and research can be demonstrated to the novice teacher. In this manner the strength of both institutions can be used to forge more effective teacher training programs.

Since the improvement of competence of the teaching profession requires upgrading of the performance of the current teaching force, greater emphasis must be placed on continuing staff development and in-service education. School-based staff development programs should not duplicate programs offered in graduate schools of education. Staff development programs in schools must be experiential in nature and must provide opportunities for the application of theory, the practice of new techniques and feedback on that practice, and coaching until new instructional techniques become a natural part of the teaching repertoire.

Teachers must take a more active role in inducting new teachers into the profession. Additionally, new teacher roles, such as teacher mentors, need to be defined that allow effective teachers to participate in the continuing development of competence in their peers. New roles should be developed to permit teachers to take on added responsibility for peer professional development while still continuing teaching.

The Schenley High School Teacher Center and the Brookline Elementary Teacher Center illustrate the steps that local education agencies can take to promote the continuing development of teachers. Such centers can demonstrate state-of-the-art practice and enable representatives of teacher training institutions, graduate schools of education, and local education agencies to meet in one place and collaborate in the enhancement of the teaching profession.

The nation's confidence in public education will be restored when competent young people are attracted to the profession, when rigorous teacher training programs are provided, and when it is demonstrated that graduate education institutions and the public schools pool their human and financial resources to promote the continual development of educational professionals. The leadership personnel of all three institutions must assume the responsibility to establish better ties among themselves in order to pursue the important goal of providing competent teachers for the nation's schools.

C. *Peter Magrath*

Robert L. Egbert

❊❧❊❧❊❧❊❧❊❧❊❧❊❧❊❧❊❧❊❧❊❧❊

Sharing the Responsibility for Reforming Teacher Education

The contents of this book have reflected our continuing assumptions that every part of a teacher's preparation can be improved; that even the best existing programs are not good enough; that teaching is a complex human endeavor guided by knowledge that is both scientific and artistic and that teachers are professionals, not merely technicians; that the education of prospective teachers will continue to be centered in colleges and universities, which provide structure for the systematic study of organized bodies of knowledge as well as the scholarly inquiry and intellectual discourse that are integral to the education of all professions; that teacher education is not a single, time-bound activity but a continuing process of career development; and that education is primarily a state, not a federal, function.

Because of our commitment to these assumptions and their implications, we are concerned about current recommendations that teacher education be removed from colleges and universities. We are also concerned about recommendations implying that the ultimate control of teacher education and its quality should be built around national tests and certification. (We do not oppose carefully developed national tests of the kind proposed in *A Nation Prepared* [Carnegie Task Force on Teaching as a Profession, 1986], but we urge that all persons committed to better teacher education remember that tests are but one component of quality programs.) Finally, we are concerned about recommendations that would remove teacher education from the undergraduate level and make it entirely a graduate program. Teachers need a synthesis of liberal arts with pedagogical knowledge and teaching skills; this synthesis is best achieved if they are studied and practiced concurrently. Thus, although we are convinced that the acquisition of the knowledge and skills needed by teachers requires at least five years, we are equally convinced that professional education should not be removed from liberal arts education by placing professional education at the graduate level.

The disparity between the percentage of minority teachers and minority students in our schools is becoming one of the most serious education issues of our time. Presidents and boards should recognize the seriousness of this issue—specifically, that attracting minority students into teacher education will require special efforts and funds. Without leadership from the president and the board in emphasizing minority enrollment in teacher education and in securing funds for minority students, the disparity will continue to increase.

The gains that good teacher education programs are making result in large part from research conducted during the past twenty years. This research was funded, for the most part, through federal programs that began in the 1960s, quickly reached a peak, and then diminished rapidly to their present low level of funding. Even in the peak years, funding for educational research and development was minuscule in comparison with what was needed and with what is provided such other fields as agriculture, engineering, and medicine. For example, education's share of the $33 billion 1980 federal research and development budget was $123 million, less than 1 percent as much as the Defense Department's share. Personnel research and development within the Department of Defense was $473 million, almost four times the amount provided for all of educational research in the Department of Education.

Unless changes are made, the subminimal level of support now being provided for educational research and development activities will continue to stand in the way of progress in education; yet none of the major national reports about education have noted this fact. Until we provide increased funding for educational research and development, we will not achieve the advances that we have experienced in other fields. Presidents should work as hard for increasing research funding for education as they do for the National Science Foundation and the National Institutes of Health; they should be as concerned about private contributions to research in education as they are to other vital research fields.

Presidents should be especially concerned about their own teacher education programs. Every president whose college or university has a teacher education program should make a careful and thorough evaluation of that program and those who graduate from it. As stated in *A Call for Change,* "If the programs are less than first rate, they should either be given the resources and leadership to make them so, or they should be closed" (National Commission for Excellence in Teacher Education, 1985, p. 23). This statement is blunt, but it was made deliberately. It recognizes our schools' need for first-rate teachers—the only kind worth having. In practical terms the responsibility for first-rate teacher education programs rests squarely with college and university presidents and their governing boards. It is they who have life-and-death power over those programs. It is they who are empowered to insist that a program be good or be closed. As responsible leaders in the education community, they are the ones who must make the necessary decisions and take the essential steps. To make such tough decisions will require fundamental changes in attitude and perception by some college and university presidents, academic administrators, and their governing boards. Nevertheless, these decisions should be made.

Just as presidents and boards must modify their perceptions and expectations of teacher education, so must teacher educators. At least three fundamental changes are needed in the community of teacher educators. First, teacher educators should become so completely convinced of the importance and complexity of what teachers do that they will accept nothing but quality performance from themselves, their colleagues, and their students. For far too long, teacher educators have settled, perhaps subtly and unwittingly, for too little. Second, teacher educators should recognize that increasing knowledge and improving technology make improvement possible in all of teacher education and that their responsibility is to apply the knowledge and use the technology. Third, and finally, teacher educators should become tougher and more sharply focused in the way they make requests of college and university presidents, and the broader society, for funds and other resources to support teacher education.

Finally, college and university presidents and teacher education faculty must make a conscious decision to work together for the reform of teacher education. The necessary changes will not take place unless the two groups make a concerted effort. If they do not, change in teacher education will be thrust upon us in ways that may well work to the detriment of all of education.

References

Academy for Educational Development. *Teacher Development in Schools: A Report to the Ford Foundation.* New York: Academy for Educational Development, 1985.

Akin, J. N. *Teacher Supply/Demand: A Report Based upon an Opinion Survey of Teacher Placement Officers.* Manhattan, Kans.: Association for School, College and University Staffing, 1984.

American Association of Colleges for Teacher Education. *Teacher Education Policy in the States: Fifty-State Survey of Legislative and Administrative Actions.* Washington, D.C.: American Association of Colleges for Teacher Education, 1985.

Baratz, J. C. *Black Participation in the Teacher Pool.* Princeton, N.J.: Educational Testing Service, 1986.

Barro, S. M. *An Assessment of NCES Data Collection Efforts in Two Areas: School Finance and Teachers.* Washington, D.C.: SMB Economic Research, 1985.

Berliner, D. C. "Making the Right Changes in Preservice Education." *Phi Delta Kappan,* 1984, *66* (2), 94–96.

Berliner, D. C. "Laboratory Settings and the Study of Teacher Education." *Journal of Teacher Education,* 1985, *36* (6), 2–8.

Berry, B., Noblit, G. W., and Hare, R. D. *A Qualitative Critique of Teacher Labor Market Studies.* Washington, D.C.: National Institute of Education, 1985.

Berryman, S. E. *Education and Employment: Substitution Pos-*

sibilities and the Teacher Labor Force: Supply and Demand. Santa Monica, Calif.: Rand, 1985.

Boice, R. "Reexamination of Traditional Emphases in Faculty Development." *Research in Higher Education,* 1984, *21* (2), 195–209.

Bowen, E. "And Now, a Teacher Shortage." *Time,* July 22, 1985, p. 63.

Bowen, H. R. *The Costs of Higher Education: How Much Do Colleges and Universities Spend per Student and How Much Should They Spend?* San Francisco: Jossey-Bass, 1980.

Boyer, E. *High School.* New York: Harper & Row, 1983.

Bush, R. *The Beginning Years of Teaching: A Focus for Collaboration in Teacher Education.* Palo Alto, Calif.: Stanford University, 1983.

California Commission on the Teaching Profession. *Who Will Teach Our Children? A Strategy for Improving California's Schools.* Sacramento: California Commission on the Teaching Profession, 1985.

Carnegie Task Force on Teaching as a Profession. *A Nation Prepared: Teachers for the 21st Century.* New York: Carnegie Forum on Education and the Economy, 1986.

Conant, J. B. *The Education of American Teachers.* New York: McGraw-Hill, 1963.

Darling-Hammond, L. *Beyond the Commission Reports: The Coming Crisis in Teaching.* Santa Monica, Calif.: Rand, 1984.

Darling-Hammond, L., and others. *A Conceptual Framework for Examining Staffing and Schooling.* Santa Monica, Calif.: Rand, 1986.

Downing, G., and Shanker, A. *Making Do in the Classroom: A Report on the Misassignment of Teachers.* Washington, D.C.: Council for Basic Education and American Federation of Teachers, 1985.

Dreeden, R. *The Nature of Teaching.* Glenview, Ill.: Scott, Foresman, 1970.

Ducharme, E. "Faculty Development in Schools, Colleges, and Departments of Education." *Journal of Teacher Education,* 1981, *32* (8), 30–34.

Ducharme, E. "Teacher Educators: Description and Analysis." In L. Katz and J. Raths (eds.), *Advances in Teacher Education.* Vol. 2. Norwood, N.J.: Ablex, 1986.

Ducharme, E., and Agne, R. "The Education Professoriate: A Research Based Perspective." *Journal of Teacher Education,* 1982, *33* (6), 30-36.

Eisenberg, L., and Grunwald, L. "A Census of America's Leadership Class." *Esquire,* Dec. 1985, pp. 65-76.

Erikson, E. H. *Childhood and Society.* New York: Norton, 1950.

Feistritzer, C. E. *The Condition of Teaching: A State by State Analysis.* Princeton, N.J.: Princeton University Press, 1983.

Feistritzer, C. E. *The Making of a Teacher.* Washington, D.C.: National Center for Educational Information, 1984.

Fisher, J. "Learning from Space." *Detroit Free Press,* Dec. 27, 1985, sec. A, pp. 1, 15.

Francis, E. Untitled paper presented at the Multidisciplinary International Research Symposium on Classroom Discussion as a Means of Teaching and Learning, Wingspread Conference Center, Racine, Wis., Mar. 1985.

Freedman, M. (ed.). *Facilitating Faculty Development.* New Directions for Higher Education, no. 1. San Francisco: Jossey-Bass, 1973.

Freedman, M. *Academic Culture and Faculty Development.* Orinda, Calif.: Montaigne Publishing, 1979.

Gaff, J. G. *Toward Faculty Renewal: Advances in Faculty, Instructional, and Organizational Development.* San Francisco: Jossey-Bass, 1975.

Gage, N. L. *The Scientific Basis of the Art of Teaching.* New York: Teachers College Press, 1978.

Geertz, C. *Interpretation of Cultures.* New York: Basic Books, 1973.

Glickman, C. D. *Supervision of Instruction: A Developmental Approach.* Boston: Allyn & Bacon, 1985.

Goertz, M., Ekstrom, R. B., and Coley, R. J. *The Impact of State Policy on Entrance into the Teaching Profession.* Princeton, N.J.: Educational Testing Service, 1984.

Goodlad, J. I. *A Place Called School: Prospects for the Future.* New York: McGraw-Hill, 1984.

Goodlad, J. I. "The Elements of Vital Teacher Education Programs." Paper presented at annual meeting of the American Association of Colleges for Teacher Education, Chicago, 1986.

Governor's Commission on Equity and Excellence in Connecticut. *Teachers for Today and Tomorrow.* Hartford, Conn.: Office of Governor, 1985.

Graybeal, W. S. *Teacher Supply and Demand in Public Schools, 1981-82.* Washington, D.C.: National Education Association, 1983.

Harris, L., and others. *The Metropolitan Life Survey of Former Teachers in America.* New York: Metropolitan Life Insurance Company, 1986.

Harvey, D. J., Hunt, D. E., and Schroeder, H. *Conceptual Systems and Personality Organization.* New York: Wiley, 1961.

Hawley, W. D. "Toward a Comprehensive Strategy for Addressing the Teacher Shortage." *Phi Delta Kappan,* June 1986, pp. 712-718.

Heck, S., and Williams, C. R. *The Complex Roles of the Teacher.* New York: Teachers College Press, 1984.

Hodgkinson, H. *The Schools We Need for the Kids We've Got.* Washington, D.C.: American Association of Colleges for Teacher Education, 1986.

Holmstrom, E. I. *Recent Changes in Teacher Education Programs.* Washington, D.C.: American Council on Education, 1985.

Hulik, K. "The Chaos in the American Classroom." *Ann Arbor News,* Dec. 1, 1985, sec. C, pp. 1-2.

Imig, D. "Briefing." *AACTE Briefs,* June 1986, p. 1 ff.

Joyce, B., and Showers, B. "Improving Inservice Education: The Message of Research." *Educational Leadership,* 1980, *37* (5), 379-385.

Kerr, D. "Teaching Competence and Teacher Education in the U.S." *Teachers College Record,* 1983, *84* (3), 525-552.

Kluender, M. M. "Attitudes of Selected Policymakers Toward Alternative Policies as They Affect Supply and Demand."

Unpublished doctoral dissertation, University of Nebraska–Lincoln, 1983.

Knowles, M. *The Adult Learner: A Neglected Species.* Houston: Gulf Publishing, 1973.

Knox, A. B. *Adult Development and Learning: A Handbook on Individual Growth and Competence in the Adult Years for Education and the Helping Professions.* San Francisco: Jossey-Bass, 1977.

Kohlberg, L. "Stage and Sequence: The Cognitive Development Approach to Socialization." In P. B. Bates and K. W. Schaie (eds.), *Life-Span Development Psychology: Personality and Socialization.* Orlando, Fla.: Academic Press, 1969.

Lanier, J. E., and Little, J. W. "Research on Teacher Education." In M. C. Wittrock (ed.), *Handbook of Research on Teaching.* (3rd ed.) New York: Macmillan, 1985.

Lanier, J. E., and others. *Tomorrow's Teachers.* East Lansing: Holmes Group, Michigan State University, 1986.

Levinson, D. J. *The Seasons of a Man's Life.* New York: Macmillan, 1977.

Link, F. R. (ed.). *Essays on the Intellect.* Alexandria, Va.: Association for Supervision and Curriculum Development, 1985.

Little, J. W. "Moving Towards Continuous School Improvement." In W. R. Rhine (ed.), *Making Schools More Effective.* Orlando, Fla.: Academic Press, 1981.

Loevinger, J. *Ego Development: Conceptions and Theories.* San Francisco: Jossey-Bass, 1976.

Lortie, D. C. *Schoolteacher: A Sociological Study.* Chicago: University of Chicago Press, 1975.

McBay, S. M. *Review of Issues and Options Related to Increasing the Number and Quality of Minority Science and Mathematics Teachers.* New York: Carnegie Forum on Education and the Economy, 1986.

McNergney, R. F., and Carrier, C. A. *Teacher Development.* New York: Macmillan, 1981.

Mangieri, J. N., and Kemper, R. E. *Factors Related to High School Students' Interest in Teaching as a Profession.* Fort Worth: Texas Christian University, 1984.

Mark, J. H., and Anderson, B. D. "Teacher Survival Rates in St. Louis, 1969-1982." *American Educational Research Journal,* 1985, *17,* 413-421.

"Maryland Survey Predicts Shortage of Teachers." *Education Week,* Oct. 28, 1985, p. 3.

Michaels, M. "A Report Card from Our Teachers." *Parade,* Dec. 1, 1985, pp. 4-5.

Miller, G. L., and Mindess, M. "Training Elementary School Teachers: Myths and Facts." *Chronicle of Higher Education,* Oct. 23, 1985, p. 38.

Mills, J. R. (ed.). *A Conscious Choice: Excellence in Teacher Education.* Grambling, La.: Grambling State University, forthcoming.

Monat, W. R. *Report of the Chancellor's Task Force on Quality in Education Programming: An Executive Summary.* Springfield, Ill.: Illinois Board of Regents, 1985.

Moore, M., and Plisko, V. W. "Elementary/Secondary School Teachers." In *The Condition of Education.* Washington, D.C.: National Center for Education Statistics, 1985.

National Commission for Excellence in Teacher Education. *A Call for Change in Teacher Education.* Washington, D.C.: American Association of Colleges for Teacher Education, 1985.

National Commission on Excellence in Education. *A Nation at Risk.* Washington, D.C.: U.S. Department of Education, 1983.

National Council for Accreditation of Teacher Education. *Standards for the Accreditation of Teacher Education.* Washington, D.C.: National Council for Accreditation of Teacher Education, 1982.

Nelson, F. H. "New Perspectives on the Teacher Quality Debate: Empirical Evidence from the National Longitudinal Survey." *Journal of Educational Research,* 1985, *78* (3), 133-140.

Neugarten, B. L. *Adult Personality: Middle Age and Aging.* Chicago: University of Chicago Press, 1968.

Newman, F., and Boyer, E. *Higher Education and the American Resurgence.* New York: Carnegie Foundation for the Advancement of Teaching, 1985.

Nutter, N. "Resources Needed for an Excellent Teacher Education Program." In T. J. Lasley (ed.), *Issues in Teacher Education.* Washington, D.C.: Clearinghouse on Teacher Education, 1986.

Peseau, B. A. "Formula Funding Is Not the Problem in Teacher Education." *Peabody Journal of Teacher Education,* 1979, *57,* (1), 61-71.

Peseau, B. A. "The Outrageous Underfunding of Teacher Education." *Phi Delta Kappan,* 1980, *62* (2), 100-102.

Peseau, B. A. "Developing an Adequate Resource Base for Teacher Education." *Journal of Teacher Education,* 1982, *33* (4), 13-15.

Peseau, B. A. *Resources Allocated to Teacher Education in State Universities and Land-Grant Colleges.* Washington, D.C.: American Association of Colleges for Teacher Education, 1984.

Powell, A., Farrar, E., and Cohen, D. K. *A Study of High Schools.* Boston: Houghton Mifflin, 1984.

Prowda, P. M., and Grissmer, D. W. *A State's Perspective on Teacher Supply and Demand: There Is No General Shortage.* Hartford: Connecticut State Department of Education, 1986.

Raizen, S. A. *Estimates of Teacher Demand and Supply and Related Policy Issues.* Washington, D.C.: National Research Council, 1986.

Raths, J. "A Profile of Methods Instructors in Teacher Education." Paper presented at meeting of the Society of Professors of Education, Denver, 1985.

Ravitch, D. *The Troubled Crusade: American Education 1945– 1980.* New York: Basic Books, 1983.

Research and Policy Committee of the Committee for Economic Development. *Investing in Our Children: Business and the Public School.* Washington, D.C.: Committee for Economic Development, 1985.

Ricouer, P. *Freud and Philosophy.* New Haven, Conn.: Yale University Press, 1980.

Rodman, B. "Black Teachers an Endangered Species." *Education Week,* Nov. 20, 1985, p. 1 ff.

Roth, R. A. "Emergency Certificates, Misassignments of Teachers, and Other 'Dirty Little Secrets.' " *Phi Delta Kappan,* June 1986, pp. 725-727.

Runkel, P. E. *Report on Eligibility for Retirement of Teachers and School Administrators 1985-86 Through 1990-91.* Lansing: Michigan Department of Education, 1985.

Sanford, N. *Learning After College.* Orinda, Calif.: Montaigne Publishing, 1980.

Schlechty, P. C., and Vance, V. S. "Do Academically Able Teachers Leave Education?" *Phi Delta Kappan,* Oct. 1981, pp. 106-112.

Schwartz, H., and others. *Schools as a Workplace: The Realities of Teacher Stress.* Washington, D.C.: National Institute of Education, 1983.

Smith, B. O. "Closing: Teacher Education in Transition." In D. Smith (ed.), *Essential Knowledge for Beginning Educators.* Washington, D.C.: American Association of Colleges for Teacher Education, 1983.

Sprinthall, N. A., and Thies-Sprinthall, L. "The Teacher as an Adult Learner: A Cognitive-Developmental View." In G. Griffin (ed.), *Staff Development.* Chicago: University of Chicago Press, 1983.

Tinto, V. "Limits of Theory and Practice in Student Attrition." *Journal of Higher Education,* 1982, *53* (6), 687-700.

Toch, T. "Teacher Shortage Realities Seen Thwarting Reform." *Education Week,* Dec. 5, 1984, p. 1 ff.

University of Vermont. *Officers' Handbook.* Burlington: University of Vermont, 1984.

Vance, V. S., and Schlechty, P. C. "The Distribution of Academic Ability in the Teaching Force: Policy Implications." *Phi Delta Kappan,* Sept. 1982, pp. 2-27.

Wallace, R. C., and others. "Secondary Educational Renewal in Pittsburgh." *Educational Leadership,* 1983, *41* (6), 73-77.

Wendling, W. R., and Woodbury, S. A. *The Future Labor Market for Teachers: Quantities, Aptitudes and Retention of Students Choosing Teaching Careers.* Kalamazoo, Mich.: Upjohn Institute for Employment Research, 1984.

Woodring, P. "The Development of Teacher Education." *Teacher Education,* 1975, pp. 16-24.

Index

Academic advising, campus-wide, 130-131

Academic majors: curriculum in, 89-91; teacher education role of, 15-16

Academy for Educational Development, 150, 151, 153

Accreditation: and curriculum, 95; presidents and, 118-120

Admission: criteria for, 68-69; to teacher education programs, 129-130

Adult development, and faculty development, 74-76, 84-85

Agne, R., 77, 78, 80

Akin, J. N., 37, 39

Alabama, teacher examinations in, 116

American Association of Colleges for Teacher Education (AACTE), 36, 38

American Association of State Colleges and Universities, 118

American College Testing (ACT) Program, 47-48

American Education Research Association, 25

American Enterprise Institute, 36

Anderson, B. D., 41, 42, 45

Andrews, T. F., 111

Arizona, supply and demand in, 38, 49

Atkin, J. M., 12

Baratz, J. C., 53

Barro, S. M., 41

Bell, T., 60

Berliner, D. C., 60, 80

Berry, B., 42, 44

Berryman, S. E., 39

Boice, R., 72

Bowen, E., 37

Bowen, H. R., 99

Bowie State College, and name change, 111

Boyer, E., 2, 108, 135, 147

Brookline Elementary School Teacher Center, and teacher improvement, 159, 161

Bühler, C., 75

Bush, R., 64, 70

Byrd, R. E., 28

California: alternative models in, 38, 56; entry examination in, 68-69; minorities in, 58; professional status in, 64; Proposition 13 in, 18; school-college partnerships in, 113, 115-116, 132-133; supply and demand in, 38, 49, 52

California Basic Educational Skills Test (CBEST), 68-69

California Commission on the Teaching Profession, 64, 120

California State University, schools in partnership with, 113, 115-116

175

California State University at Bak-
ersfield, model program at, 113
Calvin, J., 17
Campbell, A. K., 4
Carnegie Commission on Higher
Education, 2
Carnegie-Mellon University, and
teacher centers, 157
Carnegie Task Force on Teaching as
a Profession, 78, 105, 108, 120,
163
Carrier, C. A., 77
Certification: and curriculum stan-
dardization, 61; and teaching
pool, 38, 48-49, 51
City University of New York,
schools in partnership with, 115
Clinical professional studies, 93-94,
102-103, 153, 158-159
Cohen, D. K., 55
Coley, R. J., 48, 53
College Board, 44
Colorado, supply and demand in,
48
Conant, J. B., 124
Connecticut, supply and demand
in, 38, 40, 52
Council for Basic Education, 12n
Council for Teacher Education,
campus-wide, recommended,
126, 127, 129, 130, 133, 134
Council on Postsecondary Accreditation (COPA), 95, 118
Cranston, A., 39
Curriculum: analysis of redesign for,
87-96; components of, 87-94;
conclusion on, 96; departmental
development of, 131-132; and
faculty development issues, 79-
83; five-year, 6-7, 10, 49, 96,
151-153, 164; in general education, 88-89; impetus for campus-
wide support of, 124; instructional focus issue of, 61; in preeducation, 89; president's role
in, 94-96; in professional education, 91-94; resources for, 107;
six-year, 21; as standardized or
individualized, 61; in subject
matter, 89-91

Dangerfield, R., 57
Darling-Hammond, L., 40, 45, 55-
56, 138, 147, 148
Delaware, supply and demand in,
38, 39
Dewey, J., 97
Differentiation, and egalitarianism,
60
Discussion Development Group
(DDG), problems with, 25-31
Downing, G., 47
Doyle, D., 36
Dreeden, R., 80
Ducharme, E., 71, 72, 77, 78, 80,
81, 105
Duquesne University, and teacher
centers, 157

Education: aesthetic stage of, 24,
27-30; discussion theories of, 25-
31; practical stage of, 24, 28, 29;
as teaching transaction, 27; theoretical stage of, 24, 28, 31. See
also Higher education; Teacher
education
Egalitarianism, and differentiation,
60
Egbert, R. L., 97, 163
Eisenberg, L., 110
Ekstrom, R. B., 48, 53
Equity: and adequacy, 98, 109; and
excellence, 59-60
Erikson, E. H., 74
Excellence, and equity, 59-60

Faculty development: and adult development, 74-76, 84-85; analysis of, 71-86; background on, 71-
72; challenges in, 79-83; conclusion on, 83; continuing, 154-156;
and exchanging positions, 85;
and faculty needs and characteristics, 76-79; funding, 84; and induction process, 154-155; and
mentors for new faculty, 81-82,
86; opportunities for, 4; phases
of, 153-154; recommendations
on, 84-86; and research, 80, 82-
83; role relationships for, 155-
156; traditional, 72-74

Farrar, E., 55
Feistritzer, C. E., 56, 61
Fisher, J., 146
Florida: supply and demand in, 47, 48, 49; teacher examinations in, 48, 116
Ford Foundation, 153
Foundational professional studies, 91-92
Framingham State College, and name change, 111
Francis, E., 25-26
Freedman, M., 71
Freud, S., 32, 33
Funding. See Resources

Gaff, J. G., 71
Gage, N. L., 60
Geertz, C., 33, 34
General education curriculum, 88-89
Georgia, supply and demand in, 47, 48
GI Bill, 137
Glickman, C. D., 75
Goertz, M., 48, 53
Goodlad, J. I., 2, 58, 97, 101, 104, 108
Governor's Commission on Equity and Excellence in Connecticut, 40
Grambling State University, program development at, 107
Graybeal, W. S., 52
Grissmer, D. W., 38, 39
Grunwald, L., 110

Handler, H., 113
Hare, R. D., 42, 44
Harris, L., 52
Harvard University, 58, 124
Harvey, D. J., 74
Hawley, W. D., 41
Heck, S., 79-80
Higher education: analysis of teacher education role of, 12-21; background on, 12-14, 22-23; campus-wide support in, 122-134; changes in, 137-138; commitment in, 138; enhancing teacher education in, 138-142; and ensuring competence of graduates, 140-142; implementation problems in, 21; importance of, 22-35; and needs of teacher education, 14-20; and outreach to schools and community colleges, 139-140; philosophical view of, 23-25; practical wisdom in, 32-35; responsiveness of, 136-138; teacher education stake of, 1-35, 122-124. See also School-college partnerships
Hodgkinson, H., 49
Holmes Group of Deans of Education, 2, 12n, 108
Holmstrom, E. I., 48
Hulik, K., 143
Human resources, in teacher education, 103-105
Hunt, D. E., 74

Illinois, supply and demand in, 39
Imig, D. G., 36, 107
Imig, D. R., 36, 107
Internship: and attracting students, 63, 70; and professionalizing teaching, 148; recommended, 6, 7-8; and school-college partnership, 152

Japan, competition with, 124
Johnson Foundation, 25
Jones, L. B., 122
Joyce, B., 156

Kansas State Teachers College, and name change, 111
Kemper, R. E., 64
Kerr, D., 57
Kluender, M. M., 46
Knowles, M., 156
Knox, A. B., 74-75
Kohlberg, L., 74

Laboratory school, reestablishing, 147
Lanier, J. E., 2, 49, 78, 79, 105, 108
Leaders: and academic advising, 130-131; and admissions, 129-

130; background on, 122-124; for campus-wide support, 122-134; and departmental curriculum development, 131-132; for elementary and secondary schools, 3-4; and faculty responsibilities, 132-133; implementation by, 134; and personnel policies, 127-129; recommendations for, 110-162; responsibility of, 126-127; and school-college partnerships, 150-162; and status of profession, 135-147; and teacher testing, 125-126. *See also* Presidents

Levinson, D. J., 74
Little, J. W., 57, 78, 79, 105
Locke, J., 17
Loevinger, J., 74
Lortie, D. C., 57
Los Angeles, minorities in, 58
Los Angeles Unified School District, and Step to College Program, 113

McAuliffe, C., 111, 145-146
McBay, S. M., 53
McNergney, R. F., 77
Magrath, C. P., 1, 163
Mangieri, J. N., 64
Mark, J. H., 41, 42, 45
Maryland, supply and demand in, 40, 47
Master of Arts in Teaching (M.A.T.), 151-152
Mead, M., 66
Mentors: and egalitarianism, 60; and faculty development, 81-82, 86; and school-college partnership, 153, 155, 161
Methodology of teaching: and content, 9-10; in curriculum, 92-93; need for, 18-20
Michaels, M., 142
Michigan, supply and demand in, 50
Miller, G. L., 121
Mills, J. R., 107
Mindess, M., 121
Monat, W. R., 138, 141
Moore, M., 39, 40

National Center for Education Statistics, 37, 39
National Center for Educational Information, 37
National Commission for Excellence in Teacher Education, 2, 6-7, 9, 12*n*, 79, 105, 108, 120, 165
National Commission on Excellence in Education, 36, 108, 135
National Council for Accreditation of Teacher Education (NCATE), 101, 105, 119
National Education Association, 36
National Institutes of Health, 165
National Longitudinal Study (NLS), 43, 44, 45
National Science Foundation, 165
National Teacher Examination, 4
Nelson, F. H., 40, 45
Neugarten, B. L., 74
New Jersey: alternative models in, 38, 56; supply and demand in, 38, 48
New York, school-college partnerships in, 115
Newman, F., 135, 147
Noblit, G. W., 42, 44
North Carolina: supply and demand in, 49; teacher loss in, 4-5
Nutter, N., 100

O'Brien, D., 22
Oklahoma, teacher tests in, 116

Peseau, B. A., 98-99, 100
Pittsburgh, improving teaching in, 156-160, 161
Pittsburgh, University of, and teacher centers, 157, 159
Plato, 24, 26, 29, 31
Plisko, V. W., 39, 40
Porter, J. W., 135
Powell, A., 55
Presidents: and accreditation, 118-120; analysis of role of, 110-121; background on, 110-114; curriculum role of, 94-96; and programs for elementary teachers, 120-121; and reform symbols, 116-118; and resources, 108-109;

responsibility of, 121, 164-166; schools in partnership with, 113, 114-116; and status of profession, 135-147

Profession: analysis of, 135-147; background on, 135-136; and changing public view of teacher, 142-145; conclusion on, 149; institutional responsiveness to, 136-138; problems of, 144; and program enhancement, 138-142; recommendations on, 147-148; restructuring, 145-148; status of, 4-5, 64, 69, 110-111

Professional development. See Faculty development

Professional education curriculum, 91-94

Prowda, P. M., 38, 39

Quality, issues of, 1-3, 10-11

Raizen, S. A., 47

Rand Corpration, 39, 45-46, 148

Ravitch, D., 56

Recruitment, recommendations on, 66-68

Research and Policy Committee of the Committee for Economic Development, 43

Resources: adequacy and equity of, 98, 109; analysis of, 97-109; background on, 97-98; discussion of, 108-109; for equipment, 105-106; for faculty development, 84; human, 103-105; for minority recruitment and education, 107-108; need for, 100-101; for program development, 107; for research, 164-165; special needs for, 101-103; status of, 98-100

Reynolds, W. A., 110

Ricouer, P., 32

Rochester, University of, education school at, 35

Rodman, D., 53

Roth, R. A., 47

Rousseau, J.-J., 17

Runkel, P. E., 149

Sabbatical, and faculty development, 72-73

Salaries, increased, 4, 52, 144-145, 147-148

Sanford, N., 71

Schenley High School Teacher Center, and teacher improvement, 156-160, 161

Schlechty, P. C., 43-45

Scholastic Aptitude Test (SAT), 43, 44, 45, 47-48, 56, 124

School-college partnerships: analysis of, 150-162; background on, 150-151; example of, 156-160; and exchange programs, 6, 8-9; and faculty development, 85-86, 153-156; for five-year program, 151-153; implications of, 160-162; outreach in, 139-140; and presidents, 113, 114-116; role relationships in, 155-156; and student training, 63, 68

Schroeder, H., 74

Schwartz, H. S., 55, 57

Shanker, A., 47

Showers, B., 156

Smith, B. O., 70

Smith, D. C., 87, 98, 100, 101, 102

Socrates, 24, 26, 31, 62

Spock, B., 17

Sprinthall, N. A., 76

Students in teacher education: academic advising for, 130-131; admission of, 129-130; attracting, 55-70; background on, 55-58; conceptual structure for, 62-65; and curriculum issues, 61; and dilemmas, 58-62; ensuring competence of, 140-142; and equity or excellence issue, 59-60; expectations of, 57-58; and faculty development issues, 79; and faculty ratio, 100, 104, 129; financial aid for, 69; implementation for, 66-69; minority, 67, 68-69, 107-108, 115, 164; planning for, 66; recommendations for attracting, 65-70; research on, 69-70; socialization of, 63; supervision of, campus-wide, 128-129

Teacher education: in academic majors, 15-16, 89-91; admission to,
129-130; analysis of concerns
about, 1-11; assumptions about,
163; attracting older students to,
6, 9; background on, 1-3; campus-wide support for, 122-134;
changes needed in, 5-9; conceptual structure for, 62-65; conclusion on, 10-11; curriculum redesign for, 87-96; dilemmas in,
58-62; enhancement of, 138-
142; external changes for, 3-5;
faculty development in, 71-86;
faculty in, 103-105, 132-133,
165-166; five-year undergraduate program in, 151-153; higher
education important to, 1-35,
122-124; implementation problems for, 21; joint appointments
in, 127-128; liberal arts component in, 6-7; methodology and
content in, 9-10; needs of, 14-
20; personnel policies for, 127-
129; practical wisdom in, 32-35;
presidents' role in, 110-121; recommendations for, mainstream,
114; recommendations for attracting students to, 65-70; recommendations for faculty development in, 84-86; recommendations for faculty in, 165-166;
and recommendations for professionalizing teaching, 147-148;
reform symbols in, 116-118; research and development in, 69-
70; resources needed for, 97-109;
responsibility for, 163-166; science and wisdom in, 32-33; selection and entry criteria for, 68-
69; standards for, 10-11, 139,
140; strategies for improving, 36-
109; student/faculty ratio in,
100, 104, 129. See also School-
college partnerships; Students in
teacher education
Teachers: career ladders for, 60;
changing public view of, 142-
145; as considered well educated, 14-17; demand for, 49-52;
educational techniques for, 18-
20; egalitarianism or differentiation for, 60; elementary school,
120-121; examinations for, 48,
116-117, 125-126; expectations
for, 143; future, clubs for, 140;
minority, 52-53; philosophical
and political understanding by,
17-18; responsibilities of, 3, 19,
56, 148; salaries for, 4, 52, 144-
145, 147-148; and supply and
demand issues, 36-54; supply of,
46-49; working conditions for,
3, 57, 69. See also Faculty development
Teaching: as art or science, 60; nature of, 12-14; professionalizing,
147-148, 160; state-mandated
requirements for, 13
Teaching pool: analysis of, 36-54;
background on, 36-38; and certification, 38, 48-49, 51; conclusion on, 54; and demand size,
49-52; forecasting, 38-40; meth-
odological problems with, 41-46;
minority teachers in, 52-53; projections on, 36-37; recruitment
for, 55-70; reserve, 37, 38, 40,
52; sources for, 37-38; and supply, 46-49
Texas: alternative models in, 56;
supply and demand in, 49; teacher tests in, 116
Thies-Sprinthall, L., 76
Tinto, V., 64

Union of Soviet Socialist Republics,
competition with, 124
U.S. Department of Defense, 164
U.S. Department of Education, 164

Vance V. S., 43-45
Vermont, University of, sabbatical
at, 73
Virginia, supply and demand in, 48
Virtues, and teacher education, 31,
32, 34

Wallace, R. C., Jr., 150, 157
Washington, supply and demand in,
39
Williams, C. R., 79-80
Wingspread Conference on Teacher
Education, 12n, 25, 26, 118
Woodring, P., 124